*What We've
Been Told
About the*

HOLY BIBLE
*is a Lie
and
Here's the Proof*

by

Reverend Terrance J. Shaw, Ph.D., D.D., D.B.S.

(

 www.trafford.com

North America & international
toll-free: 1 888 232 4444 (USA & Canada)
phone: 250 383 6864 ♦ fax: 812 355 4082

®

Acknowledgment

Profound and heartfelt thanks to Diana, who has been my research assistant, .prn format computer technician, liaison, fellow football fan and friend throughout this arduous task and marvelous journey called writing a book. Sine qua non, Diana.

Table of Contents

Introduction

Although I most certainly believe in God Almighty and in His infallibility, because of what I believe to be false interpolations I've found in the Bible, I no longer believe today's version of the Bible to be flawless and infallible. However, that is entirely man's fault, not God's. I still believe that the original Bible was divinely inspired ad given to man by God, but I believe that it has been interpolated down through the ages until, after a millennium and a half we have today's flawed Bible. I point out these flaws, inaccuracies and errors in my book. I believe the Bible we have today has mistakes in it and it is not the same Bible that was divinely inspired and handed down to the writers of old. Most of it is, but not all of it. But don't take my word for it. I want you to look up every error that I point out in this book in your own copy of the Bible and then make up your own mind. As an example of the errors that I point out in my book, check the following two Bible scriptures (emphases added are mine) in your own Bible.

<u>1 Chronicles 21:1</u>
And **Satan** stood up against Israel, and provoked David to number Israel.

<u>2 Samuel 24:1</u>

And again the anger of the **Lord** was kindled against Israel, and he moved David against them to say, Go, number Israel and Judah.

One of the two scriptures noted above has to be a mistake in today's Bible.

The book I use, and have used ever since I became a Born Again Christian twenty years ago is the King James Version. Although I most certainly believe in God Almighty and that God is infallible, because of the interpolations I've found in the Bible, I no longer believe that today's Bible is flawless and infallible. Again, I believe that this is entirely man's fault, not God's. In spite of the doubt I have regarding the veracity of today's Bible, I still believe that Jesus Christ is the Son of God who died for my sins and was raised again. Jesus Christ is my personal Lord and Savior. I still believe the original Bible was divinely inspired and given to man by God, but that the interpolation down through the ages has resulted in today's flawed Bible. I point out these flaws, inaccuracies, and errors in my book. I became a Born Again Christian back in the early 1980s after being born and raised Catholic. When I first heard priests, preachers, ministers and televangelists talk about the Bible being flawless, unerring, and infallible because it is the Holy Spirit-inspired Word of God, I automatically accepted it as fact. Now, after well over a decade of Bible study, I believe the Bible originally was the divinely inspired Word of God. However, I don't believe today's versions of the Bible are 100% as it was originally handed down. I was never taught the flaws and errors that are in the Bible in the different Bible Colleges from which I have graduated. Flaws and errors in the Bible weren't pointed out in any of my postgraduate work either. Just because I became a Born Again Christian, it didn't mean I checked my brain in at the door. No way! I believe it is my duty and responsibility to use the brain God blessed me with to investigate things and to check them out for myself. I now believe that many scriptural references have been interpolated over hundreds of years. I wrote this book to specifically point these out. The Bible we have today is not the same Bible that was divinely inspired. As children of God, each and every one of us has a duty and responsibility to read the Bible, check it out for ourselves and then make up our own minds on whether the Bible is flawless, unerring, and infallible. This is why I also tell everyone who reads my book to not just take my word for it. Look up every errant scripture in your own Bible and then use your own God-given brain to make up your own mind.

FORWARD

I'd like to make a special mention of my good Christian friends, Mel, Dennis, and Jerry. Shortly after I became a Born Again Christian twenty years ago, Mel and Dennis baptized me by submerging me under water. After I came up out of the water they laid hands on me and prayed for the infusion of the Holy Spirit. When I saw Mel and Dennis again the following week, Mel said that he and Dennis had prayed together for me several times. Mel said that each time he prayed he got a word of knowledge from the Lord about me that said the Lord has blessed me in a mighty way, that God would use me in a mighty way to do a work for him, and one day I would be known to multitudes and multitudes and multitudes. Mel said God kept saying multitudes and multitudes to him over and over more times than he could count. At that point in time I had strong faith, but I was new to being a Born Again Christian, so my walk in the spirit was as yet undeveloped. I didn't really know what God's plans were for me, and neither did Mel, Dennis or Jerry, but every time Mel lifted me up in prayer, God would speak to his heart and tell him that God will use me in a mighty way, and I will be known to multitudes and multitudes and multitudes. Even though I didn't know for sure what Mel was talking about, I agreed with him according to Matthew 18:19, and accepted the word for me in faith that God had given to Mel. I asked the Lord to use me as he sees fit and I will try my best to be an obedient servant of God.

Matthew 18:19
Again I say unto you, That if two of you shall agree on earth as touching any thing that they shall ask, it shall be done for them of my Father which is in heaven.

I believed God had my spiritual growth and development all planned out for me, and all I had to do was respond to God prompting me in my heart. But being a new and undeveloped Born Again Christian, sometimes my mind waffled. I wondered if Mel really heard a word from God about me, or if his imagination was running away with him? Mel told me he saw me growing spiritually like you can see corn grow in the summertime. I knew Mel, Dennis, and Jerry were strong believers and wonderful role models for me, so I ended up believing it a little more than I doubted it. I filed it away on the back burner of my mind and went ahead with my new Born Again Christian life. I started intensively studying the Bible. Eventually enrolled in a 4-year Bible College, and then a 3-year Bible College. After I graduated from both of them, I went on to graduate work. In my Bible studies I came across a scripture reference in Deuteronomy that told me how to know if a prophecy is of God, or not.

Deuteronomy 18:21-22
And if thou say in thine heart, How shall we know the word which the Lord hath not spoken? When a prophet speaketh in the name of the Lord, if the thing follow not, nor come to pass, that is the thing which the Lord hath not spoken, but the prophet hath spoken it presumptuously: thou shalt not be afraid of him.

Well, nowadays my faith is strong and developed, and I know that I know that I know God is real and working in my life. Even though I didn't realize it at the time, everything has culminated in my being inspired to write this book. Initially I tried to resist it and not write this book because of its controversial nature. But (to use a double negative) this book would not not be written. The inspiration kept welling up from inside of me so much over the years that one year it all came together. I finally had to sit down and write about the subject matter and in the tone and content to which I felt inspired. Now I can see that through the publication of my book and its distribution in the United States and around the world, I will indeed be known to multitudes and multitudes and multitudes just like the word of knowledge that God gave to Mel almost twenty years ago. I give all glory, honor, praise and credit to God Almighty from whom all blessings flow. Amen and Amen!!

In Shaw's Revised KING JAMES Bible, the corrected flaws, errors, and interpolations have been highlighted in BOLD LETTERING to help you see in a glance where Dr. Shaw's Revised Bible has been inspirationally amended, compared to all the other previously printed Bibles that are flawed and have errors.

Because of Reverend Shaw's book, What We've Been Told About the HOLY BIBLE is a Lie and Here's the Proof, all of the other Bibles that you own are obsolete. Reverend Shaw, under the same divine inspiration that prompted him to write this book that pointed out and proved the various flaws, errors, and contradictions that are in the other Bibles, has made appropriate amendments to correct those deficiencies in other printed Bibles. The Shaw's Revised KING JAMES Bible is an appropriately corrected and revised Bible. Every sincere and genuine Christian will need to own Doctor Shaw's Revised KING JAMES Bible if they want to have a Bible that is free of the flaws, errors, and contradictions that were revealed in Reverend Shaw's book, What We've Been Told About the HOLY BIBLE is a Lie and Here's the Proof.

Since our Circuit, State and Federal court system cannot swear in witnesses TO TELL THE TRUTH, THE WHOLE TRUTH AND NOTHING BUT THE TRUTH, on any of the former

Bibles that Dr. Shaw's first book, <u>What We've Been Told About the HOLY BIBLE is a Lie and Here's the Proof</u>, has proven to have errors and mistakes, all the court systems throughout the world of jurisprudence need to change over to and have their witnesses swear in on <u>The Shaw's Revised King James HOLY BIBLE</u>.

If you would like to order either of Reverend Shaw's books, <u>What We've Been Told About the HOLY BIBLE is a Lie and Here's the Proof</u>, or <u>Shaw's Revised Bible</u>, for yourself, as a gift for a friend, relative, or for your clergy, just contact:

Trafford Publishing
1663 Liberty Drive
Bloomington, IN 47403
Toll-free: 1-888-232-4444 (in the United States or Canada)
Telephone: 812-355-4082
Fax: 250-383-6804
Or you may contact the publisher on-line: <u>www.trafford.com</u>

F.V. Westover Trust Publishing
P. O. Box 905
LaCrosse, WI 54602-0905 USA

Hosea 4:6a

My people are destroyed
for lack of knowledge:

John 8:32

And ye shall know the truth,
and the truth shall make you free.

PROLOGUE

Today's Bible has 66 books in it. About 40 different men wrote the books that are in today's Bible over hundreds of years. The very word BIBLE means book. The Old Testament was written in Hebrew, while the New Testament was written in Greek. The first Old Testament translation was called the Septuagint. Later translations include the Vulgate, King James, Wyclif, and there have been many more translations over the years. The Sinaitic Manuscript, a fourth century Greek manuscript of part of the Bible, is kept at the British Museum. In the 14th century, the Wycliff Bible became the first major English translation of the Bible while the King James version of the Bible appeared about 1611. Some of the original divinely-inspired books are not included in today's Bible. The books are called Apocrypha, which means hidden.

The original Holy Bible was divinely inspired by God and his Holy Spirit who caused the holy men of old to write down the words that God wanted written down. The following three scripture references from the Bible tell about how this happened.

2 Peter 1:21
For the prophecy came not in old time by the will of man: but holy men of God spake as they were moved by the Holy Ghost.

1 Corinthians 2:12-13
Now we have received, not the spirit of the world, but the spirit which is of God; that we might know the things that are freely given to us of God. Which things also we speak, not in the words which man's wisdom teacheth, but which the Holy Ghost teacheth; comparing spiritual things with spiritual.

And 2 Timothy 3:16
All scripture is given by inspiration of God, and is profitable for doctrine, for reproof, for correction, for instruction in righteousness:

The three most important New Testament manuscripts are the Vatican, Alexandrian and Sinaitic. Three of the many English translations are the King James, Goodspeed, and Moffat. The Rehims-Doual Catholic Version was issued in the year 1582 and in 1947 the Dead Sea scrolls were discovered. Some books of the original Bible were written on paper made from the papyrus plant. Wyclif completed his translation in the year 1382. Some of the copies of the Tyndale translation were burned in the city of London. The five major divisions of the Old Testament are the law, Jewish history, poetry, major prophets, and the minor prophets. The first five books of the Old Testament are called the Pentateuch, and were written by Moses, and these are Genesis, Exodus, Leviticus, Numbers, and Deuteronomy. The three books written by Solomon are Proverbs, Ecclesiastes, and Song of Solomon. The five major divisions of the New Testament are Gospels, History, Epistles of Paul, General Epistles, and Prophecy. The four books called gospels are the first four books of the New Testament. They are called Matthew, Mark, Luke, and John and they tell us of Christ. The last book of the Bible is Revelation. The time from the creation to the life of Moses was the Patriarchal Age.

Isaiah is often called the Messianic prophet because he prophesies the coming of Christ more than any other.

There are 12 Old Testament books of Jewish History. The 21 epistles of the New Testament tell Christians how to live. Leviticus, Numbers, and Deuteronomy tell us about the law of Moses. The book of Psalms, also known as the book of praises, was written mostly by David. People can find out how to become a Christian by reading the New Testament. Romans 10:9-10 is being "Born Again." The ark that God instructed Noah to build was 300 cubits long; a cubit being an ancient measure of length that is equal to about 18 inches. Noah built the ark out of Gopher wood. The first two sons of Adam were Cain and Abel. The three sons of Noah were Shem, Ham, and Japath. Peter compares the salvation of Noah by water to Baptism. Abraham was born in Ur of the Chaldees. Abraham's wife was Sara. Isaac married Rebekah. Isaac lived to be 180 years old. Jacob was renamed Israel by God. Jacob's twin brother was named Esau. The twelve sons of Jacob are Rueben, Simeon, Levi, Judah, Zebulun, Issachar, Dan, Gad, Asher, Naphtali, Benjamin, and Joseph. John the Baptist was a cousin of Jesus. His diet consisted of locusts and wild honey. He was arrested and beheaded by King Herod. Jesus was born about the year 4 B.C. in the village of Bethlehem. Herod tried to kill Jesus so Mary's husband, Joseph, fled with his family to Egypt. When they returned they decided to settle in the city of Nazareth in the province of Galilee. Jesus visited Jerusalem with Joseph and Mary at the age of twelve. Jesus was baptized by John in the river Jordan. Jesus performed his first miracle in the village of Cana. Afterwards he made his home at Capernaum by the Sea of Galilee. The personal ministry of Jesus Christ lasted about 3 1/2 years, at which point, the scribes and chief priests conspired to destroy Jesus, and Judas Iscariot betrayed Jesus for 30 pieces of silver. Jesus was crucified between two thieves. 3 days after Jesus died on the cross he arose from the dead. We can be assured to rise again after death by accepting Jesus Christ as our personal Lord and Savior. As it says in 1 Corinthians 15:22, "For as in Adam all die, even so in Christ shall all be made alive." When we accept Jesus as our Savior, then we too will rise up after our death. The Ten Commandments that God gave to Moses are included in the scripture quoted below.

Exodus 20:1-18
And God spake all these words, saying, I am the Lord thy God, which have brought thee out of the land of Egypt, out of the house of bondage. Thou shalt have no other gods before me. Thou shalt not make unto thee any graven image, or any likeness of any thing that is in heaven above, or that is in the earth beneath, or that is in the water under the earth: Thou shalt not bow down thyself to them, nor serve them: for I the Lord thy God am a jealous God, visiting the iniquity of the fathers upon the children unto the third and fourth generation of them that hate me; And shewing mercy unto thousands of them that love me, and keep my commandments. Thou shalt not take the name of the Lord thy God in vain; for the Lord will not hold him guiltless that taketh his name in vain. Remember the sabbath day, to keep it holy. Six days shalt thou labor, and do all thy work: But the seventh day is the sabbath of the Lord thy God: in it thou shalt not do any work, thou, nor thy son, nor thy daughter, thy manservant, nor thy maidservant, nor thy cattle, nor thy stranger that is within thy gates: For in six days the Lord made heaven and earth, the sea, and all that in them is, and rested the seventh day: wherefore the Lord blessed the sabbath day, and hallowed it. Honour thy father and thy mother: that thy days may be long upon the land which the Lord thy God giveth thee. Thou shalt not kill. Thou shalt not commit adultery. Thou shalt not steal. Thou shalt not bear false witness against thy neighbors. Thou shalt not covet thy neighbor's house, thou shalt not covet thy neighbor's wife, nor his manservant, nor his maidservant, nor his ox, nor his ass, nor anything that is thy neighbor's. And all the people saw the thunderings, and the lightnings, and the noise of the trumpet,

and the mountain smoking: and when the people saw it, they removed, and stood far off.

In the above prologue I have laid out a brief overview of Bible trivia and more or less the main Bible characters and sequence of events taking us from the Old Testament to the New Testament, including the death of Jesus Christ and Jesus rising from the grave on the third day after his crucifixion. Finally I quoted the ten commandments that were given to Moses by God. All of the above are what is usually taught to all of us Christians. It is rather routine and universal teaching from our clergy. But from here on out, as you begin reading and studying the content of the pages of the main body of my book, you will see that I take a 180° turn. I believe the Bible has been tampered with. When you study the contents of my book you will see why I believe today's Bible has been somewhat changed and is different from the original Bible writings that God divinely inspired. I believe today's Bible has been tampered with, and the following scripture reference tells us that this phenomenon will take place, and what happens to those who preach any other gospel than the original divinely inspired Word of God that was originally handed down.

Galatians 1:6-9
I marvel that ye are so soon removed from him that called you into the grace of Christ unto another gospel: Which is not another; but there be some that trouble you, and would pervert the gospel of Christ. But though we, or an angel from heaven, preach any other gospel unto you than that which we have preached unto you, let him be accursed. As we said before, so say I now again, if any man preach any other gospel unto you than that ye have received, let him be accursed.

I believe our church leaders in the pulpit, the very elect and distinguished teachers, have been fooled by today's Bible that has been tampered with. Either the very elect have been fooled, or they know better, yet they still withhold the truth of today's

Bible from the every day rank and file Christians that attend the churches every week. The following scripture reference from Matthew 24 warns us to be careful in the latter days because this will happen. It has taken place and it is taking place today.

Matthew 24:4-8
And Jesus answered and said unto them, Take heed that no man deceive you. For many shall come in my name, saying, I am Christ; and shall deceive many. And ye shall hear of wars and rumours of wars: see that ye be not troubled: for all these things must come to pass, but the end is not yet. For nation shall rise against nation, and kingdom against kingdom: and there shall be famines and pestilences, and earthquakes, in divers places. All these are the beginning of sorrows.

And Matthew 24:23-24
Then if any man shall say unto you, Lo, here is Christ or there; believe it not. For there shall arise false Christs, and false prophets, and shall shew great signs and wonders; insomuch that, if it were possible, they shall deceive the very elect.

Chapter 1 - The Bridge Is Out Up Ahead

IF YOU READ my book with an open mind and look up all the Bible references yourself to verify the veracity of the facts that I point out, your attitude will never be the same again about what we've all been told regarding the Holy Bible being the Holy Spirit, God-inspired, infallible, unaltered, unerring, WORD OF GOD. It is not, and I can prove it.

Before I go any further, first I want to pray for all of you who read my book. My prayer for you is the following. "In the name of Jesus, I pray that all the people who read my book will be touched in a positive way by the truth of the facts that God has inspired me to write and reveal. May the covers be pulled off all the lies that have been told to God's children, and be replaced with a new and stronger connection between each individual and the God of the universe who has created all things seen and unseen. Amen and Amen!!"

The reason why I prayed that prayer for you is because a lot of you might be like me, or like I was, as I slowly but surely learned through my many years of intensive Bible study that the Bible isn't what we've been told to believe about it. At first I resisted what I was slowly but surely discovering. I fought it tooth and nail. I didn't want to believe what I was discovering. Like Jack Nicholson's famous line in <u>A Few Good Men</u>, where he says, "You can't handle the truth," I too couldn't handle the truth. Looking back I found that I went through the classic five stages of grief. l) Denial 2) Anger, 3) Bargaining, 4) Depression, and finally 5) Acceptance. It took me years before I finally accepted the truth of the facts of my discoveries, and if you are a devout Christian like I am, I don't see why the shock to your belief system will be any different than the stages I had to work through. Of course at the time I was working through the five stages of grief I wasn't actually cognizant that the dynamic was playing out in me. It was only after I had finally come to acceptance did I look back and realize that for over a decade I had been riding the roller coaster through the five stages of grief. This is what motivated me to pray for each of you to be able to approach this with an open mind, check everything out for yourself in your own Bible, think for yourself, and come to your own conclusion.

In my mind I envision myself and all of my fellow human beings in God's creation, as being on a journey through this life, where we are confronted with lessons we need to learn as we progress. Some of our journeys are long, some are short, but we all are on the same path as fellow human beings. It is the same path for all of us, even though the nuances of each of our individual lessons come along at different times. We are all ahead of some people on the path in this journey of maturity and discovery through life, just as we are all behind others. I am presently at a different place on the path in my journey than where I was 30 years ago, and so are you. It seems that every few years as I take stock of my life, I have matured during my journey along the path. Some years the gain is almost negligible, some years the gains are baby steps, while other years I notice that I've made giant steps forward. I believe we are all inching our way along the same path of this life, individually laboring with the lessons and pains of maturity, yet collectively on the same path, albeit at different places, as we journey along from birth to death, and beyond on to the judgment we face from God Almighty at the end of this life.

I've heard many, many, many, in fact, almost all of the clergy say while preaching or giving their sermon, "If there is one mistake in the Bible, then you can't believe any of it. The Bible is flawless. The Bible is the Holy Spirit inspired Word of God. The Bible is flawless and unerring. The Bible is God's Word and God is infallible." These types of comments are routinely stated from the pulpit in churches across the United States and around the world every Sunday of every week of every year. It is stated matter of factly by the clergy, and the good, God-loving, children of God in the pews don't question it. This is the danger to us as children of God when we let a man come between us and our God and tell us what to think and what to believe. This is why at the beginning of my book I suggested that each person who reads my book should look up all the Bible references that I will talk about in their own Bible to verify facts that I point out. I take my relationship with God personally, like Abraham took his relationship with God personally, one on one. Abraham didn't have or allow a man to come between him and his God. Neither do I, and neither should you.

I became a Born Again Christian back in the early 1980s, and when I first heard preachers, priests, and ministers talk about the Bible being flawless, unerring, and infallible, because it is the Holy Spirit inspired Word of God, automatically accepted it as fact. Nowadays, over twenty years after I first became a Born Again Christian, with all the Bible study I have done and well over a decade of Bible College attendance and the courses I have taken, I believe the Bible originally was the divinely inspired Word of God. But I don't believe the Bible is now 100% as it was originally handed down. Just because I became a Born Again Christian, after being born and raised Catholic before that, it doesn't mean I checked my brain in at the door. No Way! I believe it is my duty and responsibility to use the brain God blessed me with to investigate things and to check them out for myself. I now believe the Bible had been interpolated hundreds of years ago, as I will go on to specifically point out in this book. The Bible we have today is not the same Bible that was divinely inspired. As the children of God that we all are, each and every one of us has a duty and responsibility to read the Bible, check it out for ourselves, and make up our own minds on whether it is flawless, unerring, and infallible, or not. This is why I also tell everyone who reads my book to not just take my word for it. Look it up in your own Bible and then make up your own mind. The book I use, and have used ever since I became a Born Again Christian is the King James Version. Although I most certainly believe in God Almighty and that God is infallible, because of the interpolations I've found in the Bible, I no longer believe that today's Bible is flawless. However, that is entirely man's fault, not God's.

For those of you who might not have heard of the word INTERPOLATE before, I will include the dictionary definition from my Webster's Concise Family Dictionary.

Interpolate   To change (as a text) by inserting new or foreign matter.
To insert (as words) into a text or into a conversation.

Revelation 22:18-19
For I testify unto every man that heareth the words of the prophecy of this book, If any man shall add unto these things, God shall add unto him the plagues that are written in this book: And if any man shall take away from the words of this prophecy, God shall take away his part out of the book of life, and out of the holy city, and from the things which are written in this book.

The above scripture refers to the book of Revelation, but it can also be a warning. It can be a warning to anyone who has inappropriately interpolated the writings of the Bible without the anointing of God's Holy Spirit as a guide and inspiration to him.

The primary reason that I am writing this book is Jesus' words in John 21:15-17.

<u>John 21:15-17</u>
So when they had dined, Jesus saith to Simon Peter, **Simon, son of Jonas, lovest thou me more than these?** He saith unto him, Yea, Lord; thou knowest that I love thee. He saith unto him, **Feed my lambs.** He saith to him again the second time, **Simon, son of Jonas, lovest thou me?** He saith unto him, Yea, Lord; thou knowest that I love thee. He saith unto him, Feed my sheep. He saith unto him the third time, Simon, son of Jonas, lovest thou me? Peter was grieved because he said unto him the third time, Lovest thou me? And he said unto him, Lord, thou knowest all things; thou knowest that I love thee. Jesus saith unto him, **Feed my sheep.**

God and I don't want God's beloved sheep to be led astray by ministers like Jim Jones and people like David Koresh. There are thousands of preachers, many of them mainstream, high profile preachers and televangelists, that don't even know that God's Word, the Holy Bible, has been interpolated from when it was originally given to us through divine inspiration. The ministers, priests, and televangelists either don't know or they know and they keep it away from God's sheep. In the first case, if ministry heads don't know, then they have been duped by the higher clergy who do know and are keeping it hidden from public knowledge. Those uninformed ministers obviously haven't done their own homework and researched the Bible for themselves. They probably went through various Bible Colleges and Universities, as I did, simply accepting the curriculum of the colleges and universities, blindly doing the required studies and giving the rote answers, term papers, and theses that were expected of them. Those first case ministers are probably well meaning, but nevertheless lacking in the whole truth and facts that everyone needs to know about the Bible. Those thousands of mainstream and high profile ministers and televangelists can remedy their deficiencies simply by reading my book with an open mind, looking up the Bible references in their own Bibles to verify the facts that I point out, and arrive at their own conclusions. I don't expect or even want anyone who reads my book to simply take my word for anything. You should look everything up in your own Bible and make up your own mind if what I am pointing out are indeed facts about the flaws that are in the Bible. I'm not making any of this up. It's in the Bible and has been there in the Bible all along, just waiting for you to do your own work and check it out for yourself, instead of just accepting whatever is told to you from the pulpits of your own churches across the United States and in the churches in the rest of the world around the globe.

I was never taught the flaws and errors that are in the Bible in the several different Bible Colleges from which I graduated. I took all of their curriculum, did all of the homework and assignments they required of me, yet not one error in the Bible was pointed out. Flaws and errors in the Bible weren't pointed out in any of my postgraduate work either. Why are our Christian institutions of higher learning keeping the flaws and errors secret? Christian clergy and academia have been negligent and remiss in their duty by neglecting to openly admit the flaws and errors in today's Bible. Until I wrote this book, it was up to the Christian membership to do their own Bible work and research if they wanted to know the truth of the interpolations in today's Bible and not rely on being spoon-fed only what the Bible scholars and clergy wanted them to know. Without the clergy notifying the Christian membership from the pulpit, the clergy are intentionally preaching falsehoods (lying by omission) from the pulpit to the congregations when they tell you that the Holy Bible is the infallible, unaltered, unerring WORD OF GOD. But after my book gets published and into the hands of all the people in the congregations of every church, then any minister, priest, or televangelist that preaches that the Bible is the infallible, unaltered, unerring WORD OF GOD will knowingly and intentionally, with reckless disregard, be preaching falsehoods from the pulpit to Jesus' sheep as Jesus talks about in John 21:15-17.

This brings me to the second case, those ministry heads that do know that the Bible is flawed, yet they keep it secret and continue to preach from the pulpit, teach in the Bible Colleges, and televangelists on TV, that the Bible is the infallible, unaltered, unerring WORD OF GOD. They are incorrigible, out to intentionally mislead the children of God. However, as soon as my book gets into the hands of all God's children in all the churches across the United States and in the rest of the world, the clergy leaders' secret will be out to the Christian laity. Once my book is in the hands of the laity, the ministers, priests, and televangelists, won't be able to mislead Jesus' lambs any longer. Clergy will tell the congregation everything else they have found in the Bible, but they won't tell the sheep about the interpolations. When I think of the clergy intentionally keeping the secret that today's Bible is flawed from the laity, Jesus' words in Matthew 23:27-28 come to mind.

Matthew 23:27-28
Woe unto you, scribes and Pharisees, hypocrites! for you are like unto whited sepulchres, which indeed appear beautiful outward, but are within full of dead men's bones, and of all uncleanness. Even so ye also outwardly appear righteous unto men, but within ye are full of hypocrisy and iniquity.

With all the Bible study and research I have done, I feel it is my duty to warn and inform God's beloved sheep. I get the mental picture that I am driving down highway I-40 in Oklahoma. As I'm driving along I see the car ahead of me drive over the edge where the road is supposed to be. I quickly put on my brakes and pull off to the side just before I would have driven off the road too. A barge in the river below the highway had collided with the bridge support and knocked down the bridge road, and the cars ahead of me were driving off into the abyss of the turgid, raging river losing their lives. Thank God I stopped in time or I too would have perished in the raging river below. As I pull off to the side of the road I see in my rear view mirror another car coming down the road, not knowing the bridge had been knocked down by a barge.

I quickly get out of my car, take off my coat, and use my coat as a flag to wave at the oncoming cars, hoping they will heed my warning and stop before they too drive off the road where the bridge had been knocked down by the barge. My heart goes out to the people this really happened to in Oklahoma. In my book I am using this example as a metaphor for how I feel God is using me to wave at the God-loving people who don't know that today's Bible is interpolated because their leadership has kept it from them. God's children are perishing for lack of knowledge. The laity doesn't know or realize that today's Bible is flawed. They are being kept in the dark by unscrupulous ministers, priests, and televangelists who are in the pulpit preaching that today's Bible is the infallible, unaltered, unerring WORD OF GOD. Through my book I am warning the Christians all across the United States and around the world that the ministers, priests, and televangelists are misinforming them, the same way I was waving my coat as a flag to unwary travelers driving down the highway not knowing the bridge up ahead has been knocked down by a barge.

If you attend a church and are sitting under a ministry, liberal or conservative, and your minister, priest, or televangelist doesn't know, or hasn't had it revealed to them by God and so hasn't been telling you where in the Bible there are flaws, or that God's word has been interpolated, then you need to question if you are in the right church and if your clergy is truly anointed by God. Do you really need that person to be your minister? The question is; did your minister know the Bible was flawed and has been interpolated and is purposely not telling you? If that is the case, then they are lying by omission so they can manipulate you by telling you the Bible is infallible, unaltered, and unerring. Get away from that minister. Or, did your minister not know the Bible was flawed and has been interpolated and therefore they were unable to tell you? If that's the case, it is an omission through ignorance of the Bible and through not studying and researching the Bible enough for themselves outside of their own Bible College curriculum. A person like that probably checked their brain in at the door when they entered Bible College, Seminary, or the University, and accepted everything that was spoon-fed to them by their teachers and clergy elders as fact. That omission by ignorance can be corrected. That minister, priest, or televangelist can rehabilitate themselves by reading my book with an open mind and looking up all the Bible references to verify the facts that I point out about the flaws there are in the Bible, and admit it from the pulpit to the laity. If your minister, priest, or televangelist doesn't do that, then get yourself away from that minister because if they are content to only repeat the "party line," then they don't have your best interest at heart and they aren't qualified to be your spiritual leader.

As I mentioned earlier, I have used a King James Bible for the past 20 years. Follow along in your own Bible as you read this book with the scripture references that I point out. Don't take any Bible error that I point out at face value. I'm not perfect, I'm only human and I make mistakes too. Therefore you should look up every scripture reference that I point out in your own Bible as I point out the inaccuracies and questionable material that I've found in my 20 years of Bible College study and of pouring over the Bible. None of these Bible errors were ever pointed out to me or taught to me in any of my Bible Colleges or postgraduate work. I discovered all of these Bible errors through my own extracurricular study and research above and beyond what was taught in the Bible Colleges.

The majority of the Christians today have no idea that there are flaws and errors in today's Bible. I am attempting to use common everyday language as much as possible when I write my book, because my message is primarily directed at the laity, the common every day God-loving Christian children of God. I believe the clergy should already know about the message of my book from their extensive Bible college and graduate work that's required to become clergy in the first place. Therefore my main thrust is directed at the beloved children/lambs of God spoken about by Jesus in John 21:15-17. I'm explaining my thoughts and beliefs to the laity in common and every day language as much as possible, covering the main points and revisiting them more than once in my chat with my fellow Christians. I believe making points more than once helps to reinforce the message to the receiver, and facilitates learning. I'd like everyone who reads my book to consider that I am speaking to you personally one on one, as that is how I prefer to relate. I shun large groups. I prefer to chat over a glass of iced tea or lemonade in the summer time, and cocoa or hot apple cider (with a cinnamon stick melting in it) in the wintertime. I really would like the average church-goer to understand what I have to point out in my book, because it is glaringly apparent that it is being intentionally withheld from the church pulpits throughout the United States and around the world.

Okay, after our preliminary chat I am almost ready to quote where in the Bible there are flaws and errors, which prove that the Bible is not unaltered and unerring as the majority of preachers, priests, ministers and the televangelists are schooled to tell us from the pulpits. Before I get into it, first I want to go on record saying that in spite of the doubt I have regarding the unaltered, unerring, infallible authenticity of today's Bible, I still believe in blind faith that Jesus Christ is the Son of God who died for my sins and was raised again. Jesus Christ is my personal Lord and Savior. I still believe the original Bible was divinely inspired and given to man by God, but that it has been interpolated down through the ages until we have today's version of the Bible. Having said all of the above, now I'm ready to point out the inaccuracies and contradictions I have found in today's Bible that led me to doubt its authenticity.

Chapter 2 - Who Decided Which Books Were "In" Today's Bible

IN THE PATRIARCHAL age (before and during Moses' time), I believe God Divinely inspired some people to write down his words. If we had those original uncensored/untampered writings, then I would compare it to see if today's Bible is authentic. **1) However, in 325 A.D. the Nicene Council (under Constantine) decided (for God?) that from then on, some books were "in" and some books were "out" of the Bible we have today.** Just because I was born and raised Catholic, and twenty years ago I became a Born Again Christian, accepting Jesus Christ as my personal Lord and Savior, did not mean that I checked my God given brain at the door. I did not give up or waive my right to examine and research the Bible scripture and draw my own conclusions. I'm not obligated to believe everything that other preachers, priests, ministers, and televangelists tell me from the pulpit when it comes to the Bible being unaltered and unerring. I can research it and check it out for myself and make up my own mind on the conclusions. And so can you. That is what I am helping you to do when you read my book and look up in your own Bible all the Bible references that I point out; then make up your own mind.

Back in the year 325 A.D. when the first ecclesiastical council convened (under Constantine) they took it upon themselves to make decisions over all the books of the original God–inspired, Hebrew-written Bible. They declared that some books were "in" and some books were "out." Subsequent councils also took it upon themselves to make changes and revisions. Although I believe in the infallibility of the original God-inspired Holy Bible, I do not believe in the infallibility of the Nicene Council that took it upon themselves to choose which books they let in and which books they kicked out to create the Bible that we have ended up with today. I also don't believe in the infallibility of the subsequent councils' changes and revisions either. **2) Speaking of the first Nicene Council and the subsequent councils back in those early years of the Christian church, the first Pope was married as well as many of his successors, up until it was stopped in the 4th century.**

Why the reversal from the way it originally was, to the way it is today where Popes, Cardinals, Bishops, and Priests are not allowed to marry? But I digress. Nevertheless, it is food for thought when you want to decide for yourself about the infallibility of the decisions (and reversals) made by men in the early years of the Christian church. In light of this, it is easy for me to see why there are errors and flaws in today's Bible based on the interpolations that were made back then. Since the first Nicene Council and the subsequent councils, the Bible has been looked at by many Biblical scholars. The Bible has been examined, altered, amended, and changed from one shape to another by various religious bodies hundreds and hundreds of years ago. The original God-inspired Holy Bible has been exposed to a number of revisions, translations, and interpolations by the various ecclesiastical councils. Each subsequent council alleged that there were serious errors in the version of the Bible handed to them from the previous council. **3) Hundreds and hundreds of years ago, religious leaders and sovereign rulers ordered alterations and interpolations in the Holy Bible and their orders were carried out.** Now today, here are the common rank and file loyal Christians comprised of various denominations and parochial sects, accepting in blind faith what our spiritual leaders are telling us from the pulpits week after week, year after year, in every church throughout the United States and around the world. From the pulpit they tell us that the Bible is the unaltered, unerring, flawless WORD OF GOD. It is not, and I can prove it. In the pages that follow, I am going to debunk the Bible and show you the flaws and errors. God and God's Holy Spirit are infallible. I sincerely believe that. God is NOT the author of confusion. I sincerely believe that. Therefore I believe that the original, divinely-inspired Holy Bible was the unaltered, unerring WORD OF GOD. But after the first Nicene Council in the year 325 A.D., and in the subsequent councils, I allege that the divinely inspired WORD OF GOD has been interpolated and altered. Therefore the Bible has flaws due to man changing it without divine inspiration from the original, divinely-inspired manuscript.

As I've said earlier, I use the King James Bible, which has been touted for hundreds of years as one of the better translations of the Bible. You can check out in your own Bible the various scripture references of flaws, errors, and confusion that I point out to verify the facts. It's just that I personally have used the King James Bible since I became a Born Again Christian over 20 years ago.

Any **Bold** or underlined items indicate my own emphasis added, to help you more easily see what I want to specifically point out and bring your attention to the main point I'm making. If you just patiently take your time with your own Bible, I believe you will be able to easily follow along and verify the factual truths of the errors, flaws, and confusion that I point out and have a problem with. Some of the problems I have with today's Bible are the following.

Compare 2 Samuel 24:13

So Gad came to David, and told him, and said unto him, **Shall seven years of famine come unto thee in thy land?** or wilt thou flee three months before thine enemies, while they pursue thee? or that there be three days' pestilence in thy land? now advise, and see what answer I shall return to him that sent me.

With 1 Chronicles 21:11-12

So Gad came to David, and said unto him, Thus saith the Lord, **Choose thee Either three years' famine;** or three months to be destroyed before thy foes, while that the sword of thine enemies overtaketh; or else three days the sword of the Lord, even the pestilence, in the land, and the angel of the Lord destroying throughout all the coasts of Israel. Now therefore advise thyself what word I shall bring again to him that sent me.

Well which one is it? Is it seven years of famine? Or is it three years' famine? Or are both wrong? Can we ever be sure? Comparing the above two Bible scriptures, would God's Holy Spirit divinely inspire error? Is God the author of confusion? Absolutely not! These flawed/erred Bible scripture references that I am pointing out in my book prove that the Bible is flawed and has errors in it. This flies in the face of what our clergy have been telling us from the pulpits in all the churches across the United States and around the world. I anticipate that the ministers, priests, and preachers around the world will scramble to try and explain away the flaws and errors that I am pointing out in my book in order to put a better face on it. But their rebuttal can only be guessing, assuming, and anecdote. That is not proof. The proof is what I am pointing out about the flaws and errors in the Bible here in my book. The Bible is either flawed with errors and interpolations, or it is not. I am proving that it is, and you can look everything up in your own Bible to verify the facts that I am pointing out. Any stories and speculations that the clergy may try to rebut with are not really proof. It will only be their own made-up stories and speculations to try and "make nice," and put a good face on it.

Our President John F. Kennedy was shot and assassinated 50 years ago, and look at how many conflicting stories and theories there are about that. None of them really have any proof to back up their theories and stories, and that only happened 50 years ago. So how can the stories and speculations the clergy may make from the pulpits in our United States and across the world have any proof to back up their made-up words about something such as the Bible which is over 2,000 years old? They can only pontificate their own speculations to try and make nice and save face for all the times they have been guilty of having told us that the Bible is the unaltered, unerring, divinely inspired WORD OF GOD, when I am clearly pointing out that the Bible has flaws and errors and therefore proving the Bible has been interpolated.

Sources and associated background for the following three numbered statements taken out of my Chapter Two.

1) **However, in 325 A.D. the Nicene Council (under Constantine) decided (for God?) that from then on, some books were "in" and some books were "out" of the Bible we have today.**

   a) "AD 325: The Ecumenical Council of Nicea convenes to settle two controversies: Arianism and the date of the Pascha (Easter). It adopts the Nicene Creed to combat Arianism and makes it a mandatory test of orthodoxy. It rejects anything that does not conform to the Nicene Creed. "Arianism was the teaching of Arius, a priest in the Alexandrian church. He died in AD 336, and most of his writings have not survived to this day. "The New Testament and the Nicene Creed are deeply entangled with each other. The wording and the concepts in the Nicene Creed come from the New Testament—in fact, one of the most important debates at the Council of Nicea concerned whether it is proper to include a word in the Nicene Creed that does not occur in the New Testament.

On the other hand, at the time that the Church issued the official canon of the New Testament, it customarily compared writings to the Nicene Creed to determine if they were orthodox. So you are correct if you say that the Nicene Creed proceeds from the New Testament, and you are correct if you say that the New Testament is certified by the Nicene Creed. "To put it more precisely, the Nicene Creed and the canon of the New Testament were formed together as part of the same process."[1]

b) "The Forbidden Books of the New Testament: The suppressed gospels and epistles of the original New Testament of Jesus the Christ and other portions of the Ancient Holy Scriptures. Now extant, attributed to his apostles, and their disciples, and venerated by the primitive Christian churches during the first four centuries, but since, after violent disputations forbidden by the bishops of the Nicene Council, in the reign of the Emperor Constantine and omitted from the Catholics and Protestant editions of the New Testament, by its compilers. Translated from the original tongues, with historical references to their authenticity, by Bishop Wake and other Learned Divines."[2]

2) **Speaking of the first Nicene Council and the subsequent councils back in those early years of the Christian church, the first Pope was married as well as many of his successors, up until it was stopped in the 4th century.**

a) "Married Popes/Year of Papacy/Notes:

   i) St. Peter, Apostle D.C. - 64 AD First married pope.

   ii) St. Felix III 483 - 492 Two children.

   iii) St. Hormidas 514 - 523 Married before ordination.

   iv) St. Silverus 536 - 537 Wife's name: Antonia.

---

1   Ken Collins website.

2   The Forbidden Books of the New Testament. The Marley Store website.

Sources [noted on the website for the entire report, including the popes listed above]:
Kelly, J. N. D. The Oxford Dictionary of Popes. Oxford Press. 1986.
H.C. Lea. History of Sacerdotal Celibacy in the Christian Church. 1957.
E. Schillebeeckx. The Church with a Human Face. Crossroad, 1985.
U. Ranke-Heinemann. Eunuchs for the Kingdom of Heaven. Doubleday, 1990.
A. L. Barstow. Married Priests and the Reforming Papacy. The Edward Mellen Press, 1982."[3]

   b) Married popes:
      i) St. Peter (first married pope)
      ii) St. Damascus I (366-384)
      iii) St. Innocent I (401-417)
      iv) St. Boniface (418-422)
      v) St. Felix III (483-492)
      vi) Anastasius II (496-498)
      vii) St. Hormidas (514-523)
      viii) St. Agapitus I (535-536)
      ix) St. Silverius (536-537)
      x) Theodore I (642-649)."[4]

   c) "Peter was married; therefore he cannot be the first Pope.
"It is a historical fact that St. Peter was married; this, however, did not stop him from being the first Pope. It is entirely possible that some of the other early Popes were married as well, such as the two that came after St. Peter, St. Linus and St. Anacletus, whom we know very little about. There have also been a few Popes whose wives died before they became priests and subsequently Pope. There were also a couple of Popes who were laymen when they were elected Pope, but they were not married. Since the beginning of the fourth century, most priests and all bishops in

---

3   CITI website.
4   Grossworth. Inclusive Church website.

the Catholic Church were required to remain celibate; therefore you will not find any married Popes in this time period. It is possible that some of the Popes in the first three centuries of the Church were married; however this possibility diminishes rapidly as time progressed to the forth century. The only evidence of a married Pope is in Mark 1:30 and 1 Corinthians 9:5, where it mentions Peter being married."[5]

d) "The period from Constantine to Pope Leo the Great (d. 461) was one of decisive importance in the history of the Catholic Church. Its clergy took on the character of a sacred caste and began to submit themselves to the law of celibacy."[6]

e) "A clear indication of this trend in the Western Church is found in the requirement of celibacy for the clergy, which was adopted mainly on the grounds that sexual intercourse was incompatible with the sacred character of the clerical state. Legislation to this effect was first passed at the local synod of Elvira, Spain, and taken up by the Popes beginning with Siricius (d. 399), who enforced clerical celibacy in their decretals."[7]

f) "Gradually the tradition was developing which was later to become fixed, in the West for the celibacy of deacons, priests, and bishops, and in the East; celibacy for the bishops, but marriage before ordination for deacons and priests. In 385 Pope Siricius enjoined chastity upon all priests, saying that their daily offering of the sacrifice of the Eucharist made this necessary. In 390 a council in Carthage commanded chastity for bishops, priests, and deacons. Not far from the middle of the fifth century Pope Leo the Great extended to subdeacons the rule of clerical celibacy. Late in the seventh century, in 692, a council which was esteemed ecumenical by the Eastern

---

5   Grigatius website.
6   Bokenkotter. P. 40.
7   Bokenkotter. P. 50.

but not by the Western section of the Catholic Church declared that any who wished might be married before ordination as subdeacon, deacon, or priest, but no one should do so after ordination…"[8]

g) "Except during the earliest years, ministerial celibacy was neither required nor recommended during the first two centuries of Church history. "However, it is clear from a passage in Hippolytus, written about twenty-five years later, that a change had already begun; for this writer bitterly accused his personal enemy, Pope Callixtus, of permitting twice-married bishops to retain their posts and even to marry after ordination, as if this were a practice now proscribed."[9]

3) **Hundreds and hundreds of years ago, religious leaders and sovereign rulers ordered alterations and interpolations in the Holy Bible and their orders were carried out.**

a) "Traditionally, a clear and straightforward division separated the classic four gospels, which were early and reliable sources for the life of Jesus, and the apocryphal texts, which were late and spurious. Already in the second and third centuries, some orthodox Fathers of the early church used 'apocryphal' as synonymous with 'forged' or 'false.' Today, though, it is argued that the other currents of early Christianity also had their own gospel traditions, quite distinct from those we have known over the centuries. "The existence of these early gospels raises troubling questions about the limits of the New Testament and its approved list of contents. Since the fourth and fifth centuries, twenty-seven books constitute the New Testament canon, which is the Greek word for 'rule': literally, the canonical texts are the 'regular' books. But why is Luke canonical, and Thomas not? With so many hidden gospels now brought

8   Latourette. P. 224.
9   Larson. Pp. 634-5.

to light, it is now often claimed that the four gospels were simply four among many of roughly equal worth, and the alternative texts gave just as valid a picture of Jesus as the texts we have today. When we read the gospel texts found at Nag Hammadi and elsewhere, we are rediscovering quite authentic records of the earliest Christianity - or should we rather speak of Christianities? "To quote a book produced by the Jesus Seminar, 'With the Council of Nicaea in 325, the orthodox party solidified its hold on the Christian tradition, and other wings of the Christian movement were choked off. (Citation: Funk et al., The Five Gospels, p. 35.)"[10]

b) "The first list which has come down to us of the twenty-seven books which embraces only those which appear in our New Testament is in a letter written by Athanasius, Bishop of Alexandria, in the year 367. While it was not until long after that date that uniform agreement on the list was found among all teachers in the Catholic Church, by at least the end of the second century a body of writings embracing a majority of the present twenty-seven was being regarded in the Catholic Church as the New Testament and was being placed alongside the Jewish scriptures. The latter were thought of as the Old Testament and were interpreted in the light of the former. "It was, then, by the slow consensus of the Church that the New Testament was assembled and accorded recognition as especially inspired. It was not merely supposed actual apostolic authorship which ensured for a book inclusion in the New Testament. This had an important place. It was also by the test of experience through long use that the Christian community came to recognize in the writings which were admitted to the accepted canon a quality which distinguished them from those books which were

---

10   Jenkins. Pp. 6-8.

rejected, a quality which to the Christian mind was and continues to be evidence of a peculiar degree of divine inspiration, the crown of the process of revelation recorded in the Old Testament."[11]

c) "The shape of the Christian canon was laboriously hammered out over a lengthy period, roughly between the second century and the fifth, but the most intense activity occurred in the early part of the third century. (Reference: Bruce C. Metzger, The Canon of the New Testament. New York: Oxford Univ. Press, 1987). A large literature discusses the making of the Biblical apocrypha, but chiefly in the context of those books which in some traditions but not others are accepted as part of the Old Testament. These untested works include books such as Tobit, Judith, the Wisdom of Solomon, Ecclesiastics, and the first and second Books of Maccabees. As we see below, churches have been far less liberal about accepting works on the fringes of the New Testament. ... This deserves emphasis because recent popular presentations of Christian history imply that the canon was much slower to emerge, and was largely decided by the whims of the Roman state. In this view, most of the credit or blame for the shape of the New Testament falls to the Emperor Constantine, who adopted Christianity about 312, and the great bishop Athanasius, staunch advocate of strict doctrinal orthodoxy. In 1998, for example, television's Arts and Entertainment network offered a major documentary series entitled 'Christianity: The First Thousand Years' ... In this program, it was claimed that the decisive event in determining the New Testament canon was Constantine's commissioning of fifty great Bibles for the major churches of his empire, as the bishops were too embarrassed to admit that there simply was no consensus about what books were and were

---

11   Latourette. Pp. 134-5.

not included in that collection. "The implication is that prior to about 320, the churches read an almost limitless range of works, including the most bizarre Gnostic texts, which now, tragically, found themselves condemned. This idea has become widespread in recent years. To quote a journalistic account of hidden Gospels like Thomas, 'these days, scholarly research and mass market publishing are bringing to the public ancient texts that Athanasius and other early church leaders excluded.' (Reference: Gustav Niebuhr, "Nonbiblical Texts Gain Credence, Exposure," Austin American Statesman, Dec. 27, 1997.) "In presenting his own modern pseudogospel, James Carse explicitly says that the exclusion of all gospels beyond the famous four was a direct outcome of the council which Constantine convened at Nicaea in 325. (Reference: James P. Carse, The Gospel of the Beloved Disciple. San Francisco: Harper San Francisco, 1997, introduction.) "Despite these statements, the process of determining the canon was well under way long before Constantine became emperor, and before the church had the slightest prospect of political power. The crucial phase occurred in the mid-second century, as the orthodox engaged in ever more acrimonious debate with their rivals, particularly the Gnostics, so that any text favored by those enemies was likely to be condemned."[12]

d) "In 382 Jerome left Constantinople. It was in fact at the Pope's behest that Jerome began work on a project that was to constitute his most lasting achievement: a translation of the Bible, from the original languages. Up to this point Christians had at their disposal a translation of the Bible called the Old Latin which in its Old Testament part was based not on the Hebrew original but on a Greek translation known as the Septuagint. This Old Latin version was in a great state of disorder with many

---

12   Jenkins. Pp. 84-5.

variations that had crept into the text. The Pope did not want a completely new translation but only wanted Jerome to sort out the various readings and establish a standard version based on comparison with the original languages. It was a work that would take him more than twenty years to complete, and while in Rome he finished only the four gospels. Moreover, he soon abandoned the idea of simply revising the existing translation of the Old Testament. He decided to start fresh from the Hebrew original and produce an entirely new translation. But his translation slowly caught on and gradually achieved recognition as the standard or 'Vulgate,' Latin text of the Bible."[13]

e) "That various passages were deleted, altered, or interpolated into the Gospels and even more in the Pauline Epistles is true beyond all doubt. The miracle is that so much of the original remains; and this was because the authentic Gospel doctrine continued the hope of the Church until the third century and because the rapid multiplication of copies made further evision exceedingly difficult thereafter."[14]

---

13   Bokenkotter. Pp. 62-3.
14   Larson. P. 507.

Chapter 3 - How Many Men Did David Slay

Compare 2 Samuel 10:18
And the Syrians fled before Israel; and David slew the men of seven **hundred** chariots of the Syrians, and forty thousand **horsemen**, and smote Shobach the captain of their host, who died there.

With 1 Chronicles 19:18
But the Syrians fled before Israel; and David slew of the Syrians seven **thousand** men which fought in the chariots, and forty thousand **footmen**, and killed Shophach the captain of the host.

WELL, WHICH ACCOUNT is the accurate one? Did David slay the men of seven hundred chariots of the Syrians, and forty thousand horsemen? Or did David slay seven thousand Syrians which fought in chariots and forty thousand footmen? Or are both accounts wrong? At this point in time can either one be proved right? If it could, then the other one would be proved wrong by process of elimination. Comparing the above two Bible scriptures, would God's Holy Spirit divinely inspire error? Is God the author of confusion? Absolutely not! The above two Bible scripture references prove that the Bible is flawed and has errors.

Let's read on of the further proofs I have that the Bible has been interpolated.

Chapter 4 - How Many Baths Did Solomon Make

<u>Compare 1 Kings 7:26</u>
And it was an hand breadth thick, and the brim thereof was wrought like the brim of a cup, with flowers of lilies: it contained **two thousand baths**.

<u>With 2 Chronicles 4:5</u>
And the thickness of it was an handbreadth, and the brim of it was like the work of the brim of a cup, with flowers of lilies; and it received and held **three thousand baths**.

WELL WHICH IS it? Was it two thousand baths? Or was it three thousand baths? Or are they both wrong? We can't be sure which one it is either way, or if it is actually a different number of baths. This is another glaringly apparent proof that clearly demonstrates that the Bible has flaws and errors.

Please don't take my word for any flaws, errors and interpolations that are in the Bible scriptures that I am pointing out to you in my book. Look these Bible scriptures up in your own Bible to verify the facts that I am pointing out here. Then ask yourself, is God the author of confusion? Would God's Holy Spirit divinely inspire error? Think for yourself and make up your own mind.

Don't take my word about any of these Bible scriptures that I point out to you in my book. And in the same way you shouldn't take the word of the clergy who have been telling you from the pulpit that the Bible that we have today is the infallible, unaltered, flawless, unerring WORD OF GOD either. Don't let any mere man come between you and God. My personal relationship with God is similar to the one-on-one relationship that Abraham had with God. Look things up in your own Bible and make up your own mind if today's Bible has been interpolated, or not. Don't let a man come between you and God. I don't do that and you shouldn't either. Get real with God and God will get real with you. God can give you spirit impressions in your heart about the direction God wants you to go, the same way God led Abraham in the direction Abraham should go. That is the way I relate to God. So when it comes to a man like a clergyman of any denomination, or a man like myself for that matter, I will listen with an open mind and weigh the facts. Then after I have listened, I will check out the facts for myself, and, after prayer and meditation between myself and God, I will make up my own mind. The only thing I take on blind faith is that there is a God. I believe in the same one true God of Abraham.

1 Corinthians 14:33
For God is not the author of confusion, but of peace, as in all churches of the saints.

I firmly believe the above scripture reference accurately describes the nature and character of God Almighty and what he wants for us.

Chapter 5 - How Many Stalls of Horses Did Solomon Have

Compare 1 Kings 4:26
And Solomon had **forty thousand** stalls of horses for his chariots, and twelve thousand horsemen.

With 2 Chronicles 9:25
And Solomon had **four thousand** stalls for horses and chariots, and twelve thousand horsemen; whom he bestowed in the chariot cities, and with the king at Jerusalem.

WHICH ONE IS it? Is it forty thousand stalls of horses for his chariots? Or is it four thousand stalls for horses and chariots? Or are both accounts wrong? At this point in time can either one be proven definitively right? If so, then the other account would automatically be proven wrong. However, my book is not to decide which of the errors are correct. My book is simply to point out that the Bible is flawed and has errors. And this is what I am proving. How can both flaws and errors be in a God inspired infallible (no mistakes) Holy Bible? Would God's Holy Spirit divinely inspire error? Is God the author of confusion? Of course not. What I am pointing out are simply flaws and errors in today's Bible.

Chapter 6 - How Old Was Ahaziah When He Began to Reign

Compare 2 Kings 8:26
Two and twenty years old was Ahaziah when he began to reign; and he reigned one year in Jerusalem. And his mother's name also was Athaliah, the daughter of Omri King of Israel.

With 2 Chronicles 22:2
Forty and two years old was Ahaziah when he began to reign, and he reigned one year in Jerusalem. His mother's name also was Athaliah the daughter of Omri.

WELL, WHICH ONE is it? Was Ahaziah twenty-two years old? Or was he forty-two years old? Or are both accounts wrong. If we proved one of the accounts right, then the other account would automatically be wrong. This is a confusing dilemma. Is God the author of confusion? Would God's Holy Spirit divinely inspire error? No way! Not a chance God inspired these errors in the Bible we have today. Make up your own mind if the Bible is interpolated, or not.

Chapter 7 - How Old Was Jehoichin When He Began to Reign

Compare 2 Kings 24:8
Jehoiachin was **eighteen years old** when he began to reign, and he reigned in Jerusalem three months. And his mother's name was Nehushta, the daughter of Elnathan of Jerusalem.

With 2 Chronicles 36:9
Jehoiachin was **eight years old** when he began to reign, and he reigned three months and ten days in Jerusalem: and he did that which was evil in the sight of the Lord.

WAS JEHOIACHIN EIGHTEEN years old? Or was Jehoiachin eight years old? And what is so terrible that an eight year old would think of on his own to do that would be evil in the sight of the Lord? One of these two scriptures has to be an error. Is God the author of confusion? Would God's Holy Spirit divinely inspire error?

Chapter 8 - Did Both Thieves Revile Jesus on the Cross

Compare Luke 23:38-46

And a superscription also was written over him in letters of Greek, and Latin, and Hebrew, THIS IS THE KING OF THE JEWS. **And <u>one</u> of the malefactors which were hanged railed on him**, saying, If thou be Christ, save thyself and us. **But <u>the other</u> answering rebuked him**, saying, Dost not thou fear God, seeing thou art in the same condemnation? And we indeed justly; for we receive the due reward of our deeds: but this man hath done nothing amiss. And he said unto Jesus, Lord, remember me when thou comest into thy kingdom. And Jesus said unto him, Verily I say unto thee To day shalt thou be with me in paradise. And it was about the sixth hour, and there was a darkness over all the earth until the ninth hour. And the sun was darkened, and the veil of the temple was rent in the midst. And when Jesus had cried with a loud voice, he said, Father, into thy hands I commend my spirit: and having said thus, he gave up the ghost.

With Mark 15:26-37

And the superscription of his accusation was written over, THE KING OF THE JEWS. And with him they crucify two thieves;

the one on his right hand, and the other on his left. And the scripture was fulfilled, which saith, And he was numbered with the transgressors. And they that passed by railed on him, wagging their heads, and saying, Ah, thou destroyest the temple, and buildest it in three days, Save thyself, and come down from the cross. Likewise also the chief priests mocking said among themselves with the scribes, He saved others; himself he cannot save. Let Christ the King of Israel descend now from the cross, that we may see and believe. **And they that were crucified with him reviled him.** And when the sixth hour was come, there was darkness over the whole land until the ninth hour. And at the ninth hour Jesus cried with a loud voice, saying, Eloi, Eloi, lama, sabachthani? which is, being interpreted, My God, my God, why hast thou forsaken me? And some of them that stood by, when they heard it, said, Behold, he calleth Elias. And one ran and filled a sponge full of vinegar, and put it on a reed, and gave him drink, saying, Let alone; let us see whether Elias will come to take him in. And Jesus cried with a loud voice, and gave up the ghost.

And Also With Matthew 27:37-50
And set up over his head his accusation written, This is Jesus the King of Jews. Then were there
two thieves crucified with him, one on the right hand, and another on the left. And they that passed by reviled him, wagging their heads, And saying, Thou that destroyest the temple, and buildest it in three days, save thyself. If thou be the Son of God, come down from the cross. Likewise also the chief priests mocking him, with the scribes and elders, said, He saved others; himself he cannot save. If he be the King of Israel, let him now come down from the cross and we will believe him. He trusted in God; let him deliver him now, if he will have him: for he said, I am the Son of God. **The thieves also, which were crucified with him, cast the same in his teeth.** Now from the sixth hour there was darkness over all the land unto the ninth hour. And about the ninth hour Jesus cried with in loud voice, saying, Eli, Eli, lama sabachthani?

that is to say, My God, My God, why hast thou forsaken me? Some of them that stood there, when they heard that, said, This man calleth for Elias. And straightway one of them ran, and took a sponge, and filled it with vinegar, and put it on a reed, and gave him to drink. The rest said, Let be, let us see whether Elias will come to save him. Jesus, when he had cried again with a loud voice, yielded up the ghost.

THE ABOVE THREE scripture references comparing Luke 23:38-46 with Mark 15:26-37 and Matthew 27:37-50 contain excerpts from where the sign THE KING OF THE JEWS was written and placed over Jesus' head, down to where he gave up the ghost in all three references. However, the part that I specifically want to point out to you I highlighted in bold print and then underlined the key point inside of the bold print in each scripture reference. It comes down to this. Did one malefactor revile Jesus with the other malefactor rebuking the first malefactor? Or did they both (both thieves) mock and rail at Jesus? These three Bible scripture references clearly point out there is confusion on this specific point. Is God the author of confusion? Would God's Holy Spirit divinely inspire error? Would God's Holy Spirit divinely inspire the authors to be contrary in their accounts of a specific point? Of course not. God could foresee hundreds and thousands of years in the future as God divinely inspired the original Holy Bible to be written, and see to it in advance that there would not even be the appearance of impropriety. When God's Holy Spirit divinely inspires something to be written, there is not going to be any doubt or question about it. The above three Bible scripture references clearly show confusion. And I've heard the old explanation that the clergy say from the pulpit to explain some inconsistencies in the four Gospels. They say that each individual author brings his own perspective to the table. Luke was a physician, Matthew was a tax collector, and Mark was not even one of the original 12 apostles. The clergy say the differences and inconsistencies between the Gospels are because

Matthew, Mark, Luke, and John had different backgrounds and different personalities. And I say, where is the Holy Spirit's divine inspiration in them? Are the authors in the New Testament merely writing a history of accounts that they saw and heard by word of mouth or alleged eyewitness accounts (except for Revelation)? Or is the New Testament, like the Old Testament, given by God's divine inspiration? Are the clergy saying from the pulpit that it is okay for Luke to say that the two thieves disagreed when one thief rebuked Jesus, while Mark and Matthew agree that they both reviled Jesus? How can this contradiction be of the one same crucifixion of Jesus? It cannot. Obviously there is a flaw or error here somewhere. Obviously this confusion is not divinely inspired by God's Holy Spirit. This points out even more glaringly that the first Nicene Council in 325 A.D. made errors when they took it upon themselves to decide (for God?) which books were "in" and which books were "out" of the Bible which we have ended up with today. As far as verifying the true account of Jesus' crucifixion, concerning what the two thieves who were crucified on the right and left of Jesus actually did say, whether they disagreed with each other in reviling Jesus, or if they both reviled Jesus, it cannot be proven with any certainty which way it really went. None of us can go back in time and eavesdrop on the actual conversation. Therefore, without us being able to hear it for ourself, or to have infallible empirical data to rely upon, (now that we know that the Bible has been interpolated) we are no better off than when we wonder about the confusing and conflicting stories and theories there are about President John F. Kennedy's assassination. Theories about the Kennedy assassination abound, but there is no absolute proof. Even though there is one official government version of the events, it too is questioned by many many individuals who have doubts about the government's official version that is out there among all of the other unofficial versions of the Kennedy assassination.

And President John F. Kennedy was assassinated only 50 years ago. Yet there are still many conflicting theories and stories about what "really" happened. If you go 2000 years into the future, how will people know what "really" happened to President Kennedy? History dictates that it will be the official government version that will stand alone 2000 years from now, like the Bible stands alone as the official word of what is the divinely inspired WORD OF GOD today, even though the early church decided which books were "in" and which books were "out." People today don't realize that the Bible has been interpolated and has flaws and errors. When it comes to President Kennedy's assassination, which occurred a mere 50 years ago, theories and stories about what really happened run rampant and are fodder for books and movies. Was it the Russians behind Lee Harvey Oswald? Was it the Cubans because of Kennedy's Bay of Pigs invasion? Was it because JFK appointed his brother Bobby Kennedy as the U.S. Attorney General and Bobby Kennedy was bringing heat down on organized crime? Was the FBI or CIA in on assassinating President Kennedy? Or were the FBI or CIA just in on the cover up afterward? Or both? Was Vice President Johnson involved in the conspiracy? Was it a conspiracy? Or did Lee Harvey Oswald act alone? Was there another shooter on the grassy knoll? If Lee Harvey Oswald did act alone, then how do you account for President Kennedy first pitching forward after the first shot and then backward after the second shot?

President Kennedy's assassination was only 50 years ago, and look at all the confusion we have, in addition to the official government version from the Warren Commission that says Lee Harvey Oswald acted alone. When we look at the confusion of President Kennedy's assassination of only 50 years ago, how can any clergy get up in the pulpit and state matter of factly today about the contradiction and confusion when we compare Luke 23:38-46 with Mark 15:26-37 and Matthew 27:37-50? How can they say anything about the various flaws and errors in the Bible that I am pointing out? They will sound like a bunch of Enron executives trying to put a positive spin on it. I allege that the various scripture references from today's Bible that I point out in my book prove that the original divinely inspired Holy Bible has been interpolated. Whatever the clergy may say from the pulpit about today's Bible, to try and clean up the interpolations, flaws and errors, will be as factual as someone explaining a different theory about the John F. Kennedy assassination. The facts in the Bible that I point out about the flaws and errors are the only "real" facts there are. They are in today's Bible, or they are not. Look them up for yourself to see if they are in your own Bible too or not. Don't take my word for it. I'm only a human being and, as well meaning as I may be, I sometimes make inadvertent mistakes. Anything the clergy may say to us Christians from the pulpit is only speculation to try and put a better face on it. It's as simple as that. Let's read on about further proofs I have discovered to prove that today's Bible has been interpolated.

Chapter 9 - Who Asked Jesus to Heal the Centurian's Servant

<u>Compare Matthew 8:5-13</u>
And when Jesus was entered into Capernaum, **there came unto him a centurion, beseeching him**, And saying, Lord, my servant lieth at home sick of the palsy, grievously tormented. And Jesus saith unto him, I will come and heal him. The centurion answered and said, Lord, I am not worthy that thou shouldest come under my roof: but speak the word only, and my servant shall be healed.

For I am a man under authority, having soldiers under me: and I say to this man, Go, and he goeth; and to another, Come, and he cometh; and to my servant, Do this, and he doeth it. When Jesus heard it, he marvelled, and said to them that followed, Verily I say unto you, I have not found so great faith, no, not in Israel. And I say unto you, That many shall come from the east and west, and shall sit down with Abraham, and Isaac, and Jacob, in the kingdom of heaven. But the children of the kingdom shall be cast out into outer darkness: there shall be weeping and gnashing of teeth. And Jesus said unto the centurion, Go thy way; and as thou hast believed, so be it done unto thee. And his servant was healed in the selfsame hour.

<u>With Luke 7:1-10</u>
Now when he had ended all his sayings in the audience of the people, he entered into Capernaum. And a certain centurion's servant, who was dear unto him, was sick, and ready to die. And when he heard of Jesus, **he sent unto him the elders of the Jews, beseeching him** that he would come and heal his servant. And when **they** came to Jesus, **they** besought him instantly, saying, That he was worthy for whom he should do this: For he loveth our nation, and he hath built us a synagogue. Then Jesus went with them. And when he was now not far from the house, **the centurion sent friends to him, saying unto him**, Lord, trouble not thyself: for I am not worthy that thou shouldest enter under my roof: Wherefore **neither thought I myself worthy to come unto thee**: but say in a word, and my servant shall be healed. For I also am a man set under authority, having under me soldiers, and I say unto one, Go, and he goeth; and to another, Come, and he cometh; and to my servant, Do this, and he doeth and to another, and to my servant, Do this, and he doeth it. When Jesus heard these things, he marvelled at him, and turned him about, and said unto the people that followed him, I say unto you, I have not found so great faith, no, not in Israel. **And they that were sent**, returning to the house, found the servant whole that had been sick.

WELL, WHICH ONE is it? Did the centurion come beseeching Jesus himself as it says in Matthew 8:5-13? Or did the centurion send elders of the Jews beseeching Jesus in his behalf as it says in Luke 7:1-10? Which account is right? Or are both accounts wrong? At this point in time can either one of the two be proven right? If so, then the other account would automatically be wrong. Obviously this is another flaw and error in today's Bible. How can there be even one flaw or error in a God inspired infallible (no mistakes) Holy Bible? There can't be. Would God's Holy

Spirit divinely inspire error? Is God the author of confusion? Absolutely not! What I have done is to point out more flaws and errors in today's Bible. Now let's read on for more confusing and contradicting accounts in today's Bible.

Chapter 10 - Did Jesus Speak with Pilate or Not

IN THE FOLLOWING example I will take the scripture account of Jesus being brought by the Jews before Pilate to be crucified, and compare all four Gospel accounts, Matthew 27:11-26, Mark 15:1-15, Luke 23:1-25, and John 18:2919:16, to point out the confusing versions of the same account. Again I will be highlighting in bold the parts in each Gospel account to which I want to draw your attention. Then I will give a summary of the confusing and contradictory accounts in the description of the same incident in each Gospel so you can see and compare them for yourself.

In the following four Gospel accounts of the same confrontation before Pilate, the books of Matthew, Mark, and Luke agree on what took place. But when we come to the book of John there is a major variance in one segment, which gives further proof of confusion in the Bible where one book's account differs from another book's account of the same incident.

<u>Compare Matthew 27:11-26</u>
And Jesus stood before the governor: **and the governor asked him, saying, art thou the King of the Jews? And Jesus said**

unto him, thou sayest. And when he was accused of the chief priests and elders, he answered nothing. **Then said Pilate unto him, Hearest thou not how many things they witness against thee? And he answered him to never a word**, insomuch that the governor marvelled greatly. Now at that feast the governor was wont to release unto the people a prisoner, whom they would. And they had then a notable prisoner, called Barabbas. Therefore when they were gathered together, Pilate said unto them, Whom will ye that I release unto you? Barabbas, or Jesus which is called Christ? For he knew that for envy they had delivered him. When he was set down on the judgment seat, his wife sent unto him, saying, Have thou nothing to do with that just man: for I have suffered many things this day in a dream because of him. But the chief priests and elders persuaded the multitude that they should ask Barabbas, and destroy Jesus. The governor answered and said unto them, Whether of the twain will ye that I release unto you? They said, Barabbas. Pilate saith unto them, What shall I do then with Jesus which is called Christ? They all say unto him, Let him be crucified. And the governor said, Why, what evil hath he done? But they cried out the more, saying, Let him be crucified. When Pilate saw that he could prevail nothing, but that rather a tumult was made, he took water, and washed his hands before the multitude, saying, I am innocent of the blood of this just person: see ye to it. Then answered all the people, and said, His blood be on us, and on our children. Then released he Barabbas unto them: and when he had scourged Jesus, he delivered him to be crucified.

<u>And Mark 15:1-15</u>
And straightway in the morning the chief priests held a consultation with the elders and scribes and the whole council, and bound Jesus, and carried him away, and delivered him to Pilate. **And Pilate asked him, Art thou the King of the Jews? And he answering said unto him, Thou sayest it.** And the chief priests accused him of many things: but he answered nothing.

And Pilate asked him again, saying, Answerest thou nothing? behold how many things they witness against thee. But Jesus yet answered nothing; so that Pilate marvelled. Now at that feast he released unto them one prisoner, whomsoever they desired. And there was one named Barabbas, which lay bound with them that had made insurrection with him, who had committed murder in the insurrection. And the multitude crying aloud began to desire him to do as he had ever done unto them. But Pilate answered them, saying, Will ye that I release unto you the King of the Jews? For he knew that the chief priests had delivered him for envy. But the chief priests moved the people, that he should rather release Barabbas unto them. And Pilate answered and said again unto them, What will ye then that I shall do unto him whom ye call the King of the Jews? And they cried out again, Crucify him. Then Pilate said unto them, Why, what evil hath he done? And they cried out the more exceedingly, Crucify him. And so Pilate, willing to content the people, released Barabbas unto them, and delivered Jesus, when he had scourged him, to be crucified.

And Luke 23:1-25
And the whole multitude of them arose, and led him unto Pilate. And they began to accuse him, saying, We found this fellow perverting the nation, and forbidding to give tribute to Caesar, saying that he himself is Christ a King. **And Pilate asked him, saying, Art thou the King of the Jews? And he answered him and said, Thou sayest it.** Then said Pilate to the chief priests and to the people, I find no fault in this man. And they were the more fierce, saying, He stirreth up the people, teaching throughout all Jewry, beginning from Galilee to this place. When Pilate heard of Galilee, he asked whether the man were a Galilaean. And as soon as he knew that he belonged unto Herod's jurisdiction, he sent him to Herod, who himself also was at Jerusalem at that time. And when Herod saw Jesus, he was exceeding glad: for he was desirous to see him of a long season, because he had heard many things of him; and he hoped to have seen some miracle

done by him. **Then he questioned with him in many words; but he answered him nothing.** And the chief priests and scribes stood and vehemently accused him. And Herod with his men of war set him at nought, and mocked him, and arrayed him in a gorgeous robe, and sent him again to Pilate. And the same day Pilate and Herod were made friends together: for before they were at enmity between themselves. And Pilate, when he had called together the chief priests and the rulers and the people, Said unto them, Ye have brought this man unto me, as one that perverteth the people: and, behold, I, having examined him before you, have found no fault in this man touching those things whereof ye accuse him: No, nor yet Herod: for I sent you to him; and, lo, nothing worthy of death is done unto him. I will therefore chastise him, and release him. (For of necessity he must release one unto them at the feast.) And they cried out all at once, saying, Away with this man, and release unto us Barabbas: (Who for a certain sedition made in the city, and for murder, was cast into prison.) Pilate therefore, willing to release Jesus, spake again to them. But they cried, saying, Crucify him, crucify him. And he said unto them the third time, Why, what evil hath he done? I have found no cause of death in him: I will therefore chastise him, and let him go. And they were instant with loud voices, requiring that he might be crucified. And the voices of them and of the chief priests prevailed. And Pilate gave sentence that it should be as they required. And he released to them him that for sedition and murder was cast into prison, whom they had desired; but he delivered Jesus to their will.

With John 18:29 through 19:16
Pilate then went out unto them, and said, What accusation bring ye against this man? They answered and said unto him, If he were not a malefactor, we would not have delivered him up unto thee. Then said Pilate unto them, Take ye him, and judge him according to your law. The Jews therefore said unto him, It is not lawful for us to put any man to death: That the saying of Jesus

might be fulfilled, which he spake, signifying what death he should die. **Then Pilate entered into the judgment hall again, and called Jesus, and said unto him, Art thou King of the Jews? Jesus answered him, Sayest thou this thing of thyself, or did others tell it thee of me? Pilate answered, Am I a Jew? Thine own nation and the chief priests have delivered thee unto me: what hast thou done? Jesus answered, My kingdom is not of this world: if my kingdom were of this world, then would my servants fight, that I should not be delivered to the Jews: but now is my kingdom not from hence.**

Pilate therefore said unto him, art thou a king then? Jesus answered, Thou sayest that I am a king. To this end was I born, and for this cause came I into the world, that I should bear witness unto the truth. Every one that is of the truth heareth my voice. Pilate saith unto him, What is truth? And when he said this, he went out again unto the Jews, and saith unto them, I find in him no fault at all. But ye have a custom, that I should release unto you one at the passover: will ye therefore that I release unto you the King of the Jews? Then cried they all again, saying, Not this man, but Barabbas. Now Barabbas was a robber. Then Pilate therefore took Jesus, and scourged him. And the soldiers platted a crown of thorns, and put it on his head, and they put on him a purple robe, And said, Hail, King of the Jews! and they smote him with their hands. Pilate therefore went forth again, and saith unto them, Behold, I bring him forth to you, that ye may know that I find no fault in him. Then came Jesus forth, wearing the crown of thorns, and the purple robe. And Pilate saith unto them, Behold the man! When the chief priests therefore and officers saw him, they cried out, saying, Crucify him, crucify him. Pilate saith unto them, Take ye him, and crucify him: for I find no fault in him. The Jews answered him, We have a law, and by our law he ought to die, because he made himself the Son of God. When Pilate therefore heard that saying, he was the more afraid; **And went again into the judgment hall, and saith unto**

Jesus, Whence art thou? But Jesus gave him no answer. Then saith Pilate unto him, Speakest thou not unto me? knowest thou not that I have power to crucify thee, and have power to release thee? Jesus answered, Thou couldest have no power at all against me, except it were given thee from above: therefore he that delivered me unto thee hath the greater sin. And from thenceforth Pilate sought to release him: but the Jews cried out, saying, If thou let this man go, thou art not Caesar's friend: whosoever maketh himself a king speaketh against Caesar. When Pilate therefore heard that saying, he brought Jesus forth, and sat down in the judgment seat in a place that is called the Pavement, but in Hebrew, Gabbatha. And it was the preparation of the passover, and about the sixth hour: and he saith unto the Jews, Behold your King! But they cried out, Away with him, away with him, crucify him. Pilate saith unto them, Shall I crucify your King? The chief priests answered, We have no king but Caesar. Then delivered he him therefore unto them to be crucified. And they took Jesus, and led him away.

Okay, the above four references from the Bible give the four Gospel accounts for the period from when Jesus was first brought before Pilate and questioned, up through Jesus being delivered to be crucified. The first three accounts clearly state that when Pilate questioned Jesus as to if he were the king of the Jews, Jesus responded by saying, "Thou sayest it." But when we come to the Gospel of John, John's account quotes Jesus and Pilate having a rather extensive dialog back and forth. You can look up in your own Bible to see that the four Gospels are exactly as I am quoting here. If your Bible has the same accounts quoted in the four Gospels as I have quoted, then which one is accurate? Matthew, Mark, and Luke are pretty much in agreement about what happened in the conversation between Pilate and Jesus, while John's account varies widely in the dialog they had between each other. Which is right? How can we be sure? God is not the author of confusion (1 Corinthians 14:33). Did Jesus make one short statement, saying, "Thou sayest it," and then never answer another word after that, as it says in Matthew, Mark, and Luke? Or is the back and forth dialog that is quoted in John the real truth? And if that isn't confusing enough, whose men really did put a royal robe on Jesus? Was it Herod's men as it says in Luke 23:11? Or was it Pilate's men as it says in John 19:1-3?

I can't be certain which version is true. However, I can be certain (and so can you) that this confusion and contradiction proves that today's Bible has been interpolated. God is not the author of confusion. God's Holy Spirit did not divinely inspire differing accounts of the same event. Therefore I have to submit the above scripture references from the Gospels as further proof that today's Bible has flaws and errors in it. Let's read on and see where there are more flaws, errors, and confusion in the Bible.

Chapter 11 - How Many Suns Does Our Solar System Have

Genesis 1:14-19
And God said, Let there be lights in the firmament of the heaven to divide the day from the night; and let them be for signs, and for seasons, and for days, and years: And let them be for lights in the firmament of the heaven to give light upon the earth: and it was so. **And God made two great lights;** the greater light to rule the day, and the lesser light to rule the night: he made the stars also. And God set them in the firmament of the heaven to give light upon the earth, And to rule over the day and over the night, and to divide the light from the darkness: and God saw that it was good. And the evening and the morning were the fourth day,

And Genesis 1:1-5
In the beginning God created the heaven and the earth. And the earth was without form, and void; and darkness was upon the face of the deep. And the Spirit of God moved upon the face of the waters. And God said, Let there be light: and there was light. And God saw the light, that it was good: and God divided the light from the darkness. And God called the light Day, and the

darkness he called Night, And the evening and the morning were the first day.

I WILL ONLY briefly mention the more obvious point that God created light out of the darkness in Genesis 1:1-5, yet God didn't create the sun until Genesis 1:14-19. I'm not one to say what God can and can't do. God is the Supreme Being and God Almighty can do things that I can't comprehend, so it's not for me to say he can't create light before he created the sun. I'm simply pointing out that in the book of Genesis the light was created on the first day and the sun wasn't created until the fourth day. I'm pointing it out, but not making a judgment call on God's ability to do so.

The main issue I want to point out to you is contained in the part of Genesis 1:14-19 where I put in bold highlights where it states, "And God made two great lights..." As I continue to point out for emphasis, God is not the author of confusion. God knows the beginning from the end even before God creates it. For instance, I believe God knew all about DNA before He started creating anything in Genesis Chapter 1, even though we humans have only discovered DNA and its controlling functions relatively recently. God's Holy Spirit wouldn't divinely inspire error. Back when the Bible was written, people didn't know science and astronomy like we do today due to our scientific advances. But God knew everything long before today's human beings discovered them. Therefore God knows everything that there is to know about astronomy, since God created astronomy and everything else. This is another reason why I believe today's Bible has been interpolated. Why would God's Holy Spirit divinely inspire the Holy Bible to say there are "two" great lights (the sun and the moon) when we know now that there is only one great light, the sun, and the moon is only a reflection of the sun's rays and not a "light" in itself at all?

I believe that type of error is not something God's Holy Spirit would divinely inspire to be written down in the Bible. It's a blatant error to say there are two great lights when in fact there is only one great light. Therefore I allege that this is another flaw and error among the various confusing comments and contradictions that are in today's Bible. Now I will move on to point out another error I have discovered in the Bible.

Chapter 12 - Did God Miraculously Make the Sun Stand Still

Joshua 10:5-14

Therefore the five kings of the Amorites, the king of Jerusalem, the king of Hebron, the king of Jarmuth, the king of Lachish, the king of Eglon, gathered themselves together, and went up, they and all their hosts, and encamped before Gibeon, and made war against it. And the men of Gibeon sent unto Joshua to the camp to Gilgal, saying, Slack not thy hand from thy servants; come up to us quickly, and save us, and help us: for all the kings of the Amorites that dwell in the mountains are gathered together against us. So Joshua ascended from Gilgal, he, and all the people of war with him, and all the mighty men of valour. And the Lord said unto Joshua, Fear them not: for I have delivered them into thine hand; there shall not a man of them stand before thee. Joshua therefore came unto them suddenly, and went up from Gilgal all night. And the Lord discomfited them before Israel, and slew them with a great slaughter at Gibeon, and chased them along the way that goeth up to Bethhoron, and smote them to Azekah, and unto Makkedah. And it came to pass, as they fled from before Israel, and were in the going down to Bethhoron, that the Lord cast down great stones from heaven upon them unto

Azekah, and they died: they were more which died with hailstones than they whom the children of Israel slew with the sword. **Then spake Joshua to the Lord in the day when the Lord delivered up the Amorites before the children of Israel, and he said in the sight of Israel, Sun, stand thou still upon Gibeon; and thou, Moon in the valley of Ajalon. And the sun stood still, and the moon stayed, until the people had avenged themselves upon their enemies. Is not this written in the book of Jasher? So the sun stood still in the midst of heaven, and hasted not to go down a whole day.** And there was no day like that before it or after it, that the Lord hearkened unto the voice of a man: for the Lord fought for Israel.

THE ABOVE SCRIPTURE reference in Joshua 10:5-14 describes a battle of the Amorite kings against the men of Gibeon. The Amorite kings were winning the battle, so the men of Gibeon sent for Joshua to bring his army and help save the men of Gibeon, which Joshua does. The part I highlighted in bold is the part with which I have a problem. In that part Joshua asked God to make the sun stand still, apparently so Joshua and his army would have more daylight to finish the battle since the tide had turned in their favor. According to what is in the Bible, God granted their request and suspended the laws of nature, and caused the sun to stand still, which gave Joshua more daylight to finish the battle and prevail. However, God is not the author of confusion. God's Holy Spirit would not divinely inspire error to be written down in the Holy Bible. Back when the Bible was written, people didn't understand science and astronomy like we do today as a result of our scientific advances during the past 2000 years. Nowadays we know that the sun always stands still, and it is planet earth that orbits around the sun. Therefore, this is another technical flaw in today's Bible and I don't believe God would divinely inspire flaws and confusion. God knew way back then that the sun always stood still because God created the sun and the planets that orbit around the sun.

The above scripture reference in Joshua 10:5-14 is not the only place in the Bible where I have found it mentioned that the sun stood still. In your own Bible check out the following scripture and you will see it again.

Habakkuck 3:11
The sun and moon stood still in their habitation: at the light of thine arrows they went, and at the shining of thy glittering spear.

I have a serious problem with the Bible stating that the sun stood still. As I've said, nowadays we know that the sun is always standing still. Either that part has been interpolated from what the original divinely inspired Holy Bible stated, or when the first Nicene Council met in the year 325 A.D. and decided which books were "in" the Bible and which books were "out" of the Bible, they made the error of including a book in today's Bible that wasn't divinely inspired. It leads me to wonder which other divinely inspired Bible books they decided were "out" of today's Bible. I shudder to imagine.

I have no problem with an account in the Bible stating that God suspended the normal laws of nature, as a miracle. After all, God is God, and God can do whatever God deems appropriate. Notice in the following scripture reference in 2 Kings 20 that God seems to suspend the natural laws of nature as a miracle sign.

2 Kings 20:9-11
And Isaiah said, This sign shalt thou have of the Lord, that the Lord will do the thing that he hath spoken: shall the shadow go forward ten degrees, or go back ten degrees? And Hezekiah answered, It is a light thing for the shadow to go down ten degrees: nay, but let the shadow return backward ten degrees. And Isaiah the prophet cried unto the Lord: and he brought the shadow ten degrees backward, by which it had gone down in the dial of Ahaz.

A miracle like the one stated in 2 Kings 20:9-11 is not a flaw or error as stated. Since we know the sun stands still and the earth orbits around, apparently God could handle that miracle in a number of ways, or ways that I can't begin to imagine. God could have repositioned the earth and compensated for the centrifugal force that would have caused tidal waves, etc., or God could have simply manipulated the shadow without repositioning the earth in relation to the sun. Or God could have done it in some other way that I can't imagine. However God did the miracle recounted in 2 Kings 20:9-11, there is not a flaw or error in the account. A miracle stated as such is something that as a Christian I take on faith. This account doesn't state that the sun stood still like it states in Joshua 10:5-14 and Habakkuck 3:11, which in reality is no miracle at all, but a flawed or erroneous statement since we know nowadays that the earth has always orbited around the stationary sun. Let's read on to see more flaws and confusion that I have discovered in the Bible.

Chapter 13 - Who Really Wrote the Gospel of Matthew

Matthew 9:9
And Jesus passed forth from thence, **he saw a man, named Matthew, sitting at he receipt of custom: and he saith unto him, Follow me. And he arose, and followed him.**

THE PROBLEM I have with Matthew 9:9 is that if Matthew wrote the book of Matthew, then why did he speak of himself in the third person? A natural way to write about this event would be to write it in the first person if it was Matthew who was writing. This type of flaw is different than the other flaws that I've pointed out to you up to this point. This type of flaw brings into question whether Matthew actually did write the book of Matthew, or not. If Matthew were writing about an incident involving himself, he would write it in such a way as to say that this was how Jesus came across him one day, and he would own that he was talking about himself. For example, if Matthew were the author of Matthew 9:9, he would most likely say it in the following way.

"As I was sitting at the receipt of custom, Jesus passed by. He saw me and told me to follow him. So I followed him."
However, by the way Matthew 9:9 is worded in the third person,

it gives us a clue that it possibly wasn't Matthew who wrote it. Although this confusion is not necessarily glaringly apparent enough that I will say directly that it is an error (at least not as glaringly apparent as the other flaws and errors that I have thus far pointed out) I believe I am on solid ground to use this verse in Matthew to question if Matthew actually wrote it. Based on the above premise, I believe I have very good grounds to question it, although I am not able to draw an absolute conclusion beyond simple suspicion about whether Matthew actually was the author of the book of Matthew. Now the next flaw that I point out is of the same nature as Matthew 9:9, but it is even more apparent the verse wasn't written by the author to whom it is universally credited. Read on to see the flaw that I have discovered in the scripture reference from Deuteronomy.

Deuteronomy 34:1-12
And Moses went up from the plains of Moab unto the mountain of Nebo, to the top of Pisgah, that is over against Jericho. And the Lord shewed him all the land of Gilead, unto Dan, And all Naphtali, and the land of Ephraim, and Manasseh, and all the land of Judah, unto the utmost sea, And the south, and the plain of the valley of Jericho, the city of palm trees, unto Zoar. And the Lord said unto him, This is the land which I sware unto Abraham, unto Isaac, and unto Jacob, saying, I will give it unto thy seed: I have caused thee to see it with thine eyes, but thou shalt not go over thither. So Moses the servant of the Lord died there in the land of Moab, according to the word of the Lord. And he buried him in a valley in the land of Moab, over against Bethpeor: but no man knoweth of his sepulchre unto this day. And Moses was an hundred and twenty years old when he died; his eye was not dim, nor his natural force abated. And the children of Israel wept for Moses in the plains of Moab thirty days: so the days of weeping and mourning for Moses were ended. And Joshua the son of Nun was full of the spirit of wisdom; for Moses had laid his hands upon him: and the children of Israel hearkened unto him, and did as

the Lord commanded Moses. And there arose not a prophet since in Israel like unto Moses, whom the Lord knew face to face. In all the signs and wonders, which the Lord sent him to do in the land of Egypt to Pharaoh, and to all his servants, and to all his land, And in all that mighty hand, and in all the great terror which Moses shewed in the sight of all Israel.

All the Bible Colleges teach that Moses is said to have written the first 5 books of the Bible (known as the Pentateuch). If this is true, then how did Moses write the last chapter of the 5th book, Deuteronomy 34? Chapter 34 of Deuteronomy is written "about" Moses, not "by" Moses. The first 4 verses are about Moses in the period leading up to his death. The last 8 verses are written about what took place after Moses died. It's obvious that Moses couldn't have written the last chapter of Deuteronomy. Now this isn't necessarily a bad thing. Where the rub comes in is "who" actually did write chapter 34, when all of it is attributed to Moses? Once the hypothesis is taken this far, then it further brings into question who "really" wrote what books that are in today's Bible? When the accumulation of proof that I am pointing out in my book are looked at as part of the BIG PICTURE, it gives even more credibility to the allegations that are the premise of my book and which underlie my book's title: <u>What We've Been Told About the HOLY BIBLE is a Lie and Here's the Proof</u>. Now I will point out another problem that I have discovered in today's Bible.

Chapter 14 - Was Isaac Abraham's Only Son From His Bowels

Compare Genesis 15:2-4
And Abram said, Lord God, what will thou give me, seeing I go childless, and the steward of my house is this Eliezer of Damascus? And Abram said, Behold, to me thou hast given no seed: and, lo, one born in my house is mine heir. And, behold, the word of the Lord came unto him, saying, This shall not be thine heir: **but he that shall come forth out of thine own bowels shall be thine heir.**

And Genesis 16:3-4
And Sarai Abram's wife took Hagar her maid the Egyptian, after Abram had dwelt ten years in the land of Canaan, and gave her to her husband Abram to be his wife. And he went in unto Hagar, and she conceived: and when she saw that she had conceived, her mistress was despised in her eyes.

And Genesis 16:15-16
And Hagar bare Abram a son: and Abram called his son's name, which Hagar bare, Ishmael. And Abram was fourscore and six years old, when Hagar bare Ishmael to Abram.

And Genesis 17:1-4

And when Abram was ninety years old and nine, the Lord appeared to Abram, and said unto him, I am the Almighty God; walk before me, and be thou perfect. And I will make my covenant between me and thee, and will multiply thee exceedingly. And Abram fell on his face: and God talked with him, saying, As for me, behold, my covenant is with thee, and thou shalt be a father of many nations.

And Genesis 17:19-20

And God said, Sarah thy wife shall bear thee a son indeed; and thou shalt call his name Isaac: and I will establish my covenant with him for an everlasting covenant, and with his seed after him. And as for Ishmael, I have heard thee: Behold, I have blessed him, and will make him fruitful, and will multiply him exceedingly; twelve princes shall he beget, and I will make him a great nation.

And Genesis 17:24-27

And Abraham was ninety years old and nine, when he was circumcised in the flesh of his foreskin. And Ishmael his son was thirteen years old, when he was circumcised in the flesh of his foreskin. In the selfsame day was Abraham circumcised, and Ishmael his son. And all the men of his house, born in the house, and bought with money of the stranger, were circumcised with him.

And Genesis 22:2

And he said, **Take now thy son, thine <u>only</u> son Isaac**, whom thou lovest, and get thee into the land of Moriah; and offer him there for a burnt offering upon one of the mountains which I will tell thee of.

<u>And finally, Hebrews 11:17</u>
By faith Abraham, when he was tried, **offered up Isaac:** and he that had received the promises **offered up his <u>only</u> begotten son.**

IN THE ABOVE scripture references, we see that at the end of Genesis 15:2-4 that when Abram complained to God about not having a child of his own, God promised Abram a child "**that shall come forth out of thine own bowels...** ." We see in Genesis 16:3-4 that Abram's wife Sarai gave Abram her maid, Hagar, to also be Abram's wife, and Hagar conceived a child with Abram. In Genesis 16:15-16 we see that Hagar bore Abram a son, and he was named Ishmael. At that time Abram was 86 years old. In Genesis 17:1-4 we read that when Abram was 99 years old, the Lord told Abram he would multiply Abram exceedingly and he would be the father of many nations. In Genesis 17:19-20 we see God tell Abraham that his first wife, Sarah, will also bear him a son, and this son's name shall be Isaac. Genesis 17:20 shows that Abraham loved Ishmael too by praying to God for Ishmael's welfare; wherein God responds by saying he heard Abraham's prayer for Ishmael. God says he established his covenant with Isaac and would also bless Ishmael and multiply Ishmael exceedingly, as Ishmael shall have twelve princes begotten of him and God will make of Ishmael a great nation too. In Genesis 17:24-27 we see that at age 99 Abraham was circumcised, and 13 year-old Ishmael was also circumcised. So we know that Ishmael still lived with Abraham in Abraham's house at least up to age 13. All this is Biblical history of what took place, and I don't see any flaws or errors in any of it up to this point. We can still understand the chronological sequence of events as we see what came first and second, using Abraham's stated age for a guideline as accounts unfold. However, I do have a problem with both Genesis 22:2 and Hebrews 11:17 saying that Isaac is Abraham's **only** son from his bowels. The Bible documents that Ishmael was Abraham's firstborn son from his bowels, and Isaac was his second-born son from his bowels. God is not the author of confusion, and it is confusing to see Genesis 22:2 and Hebrews 11:17 both say that Isaac is Abraham's <u>only</u> son. Here again is confusion to deal with in today's Bible. However, if you take the chronological sequence of events as they unfolded in Abraham's life, there is no denying the fact that Isaac was not Abraham's only son. Isaac was Abraham's second son. These are the concrete facts. Any other explanation that a clergyman may make is only conjecture and speculation in an attempt to explain away another flaw in the Bible. It is easy to see when you follow the Bible text that Ishmael not only also came out of Abraham's bowels too, but Ishmael was Abraham's firstborn son, as God said would happen in Genesis 15:2-4. Therefore Isaac is not Abraham's only son as today's Bible erroneously says in Genesis 22:2 and Hebrews 11:17.

The identification of Ishmael as Abraham's only begotten son before the birth of Isaac is proven by Biblical evidence if we look for it. Not only does the Bible state that Ishmael was the firstborn son from Abram's bowels before Isaac, but it also says that Ishmael's mother, Hagar, was his legal second wife, in a marriage approved of and arranged by Sarah, and not Abram's concubine. This is stated in Genesis 16:1-3.

<u>Genesis 16:1-3</u>
Now Sarai Abram's wife bare him no children: and she had an handmaid, an Egyptian, whose name was Hagar. And Sarai said unto Abram, Behold now, the Lord hath restrained me from bearing: I pray thee, go in unto my maid; it may be that I may obtain children by her. And Abram hearkened to the voice of Sarai. And Sarai Abraham's wife took Hagar her maid the Egyptian, after Abram had dwelt ten years in the land of Canaan, and gave her to her husband Abram to be his wife.

Genesis 16:1-3 clearly states that Hagar was Abram's wife and not his concubine.

Whoever listed the sons of Abraham from his wives even put it backwards in 1 Chronicles 1:28.

1 Chronicles 1:28
The sons of Abraham; Isaac, and Ishmael.

However, if one will take the time to read 1 Chronicles 1:1-34, you will see that the chronological sequence of births does list Ishmael's sons in verse 29, and Isaac's sons are listed later in verse 34. In light of this, why is verse 28 chronologically misstated by listing Isaac first before Ishmael? Since God is not the author of confusion, I don't believe it was God's Holy Spirit that divinely inspired it to be listed inaccurately. I believe it was interpolated by a man who was not divinely inspired who wrote it backwards in verse 28, while the rest of 1 Chronicles 1:29-34 is listed in correct chronological sequence. Who did that? God would not confuse the chronological sequence anywhere, but it is especially suspicious and ironic to see it confused in verse 28 in a book named, "Chronicles." Because of this confusion, I don't see God's hand in it, but man's interpolation of the original text.

Now I will point out a few more scripture references that are simply confusing and contradictory. These are more proof why I believe that either the original Holy Bible has been incorrectly interpolated, or that these particular recorded scripture references were not divinely inspired by God's Holy Spirit.

Chapter 15 - Is God the Author of Confusion

SINCE GOD ALWAYS was and always will be, then the divine Holy Spirit inspiration that God sent to the writers of the original Bible over hundreds of years as the original books of the Bible were written was not lost on God and God's Holy Spirit. Or to put it another way, God didn't forget what he inspired to be said in one book of the Bible when he was inspiring another text of the Bible to be written later, even if a hundred or more years had passed. What God says stands absolute, and since God is not the author of confusion, he would not say one thing in one of his inspired writings, and then say the opposite in another divinely inspired writing. Let's take a look at the following scripture reference for another example. After all, all we have to go by today that are an undisputed fact are the scriptures.

Compare John 1:18
No man hath seen God at any time; the only begotten Son, which is in the bosom of the Father, he hath declared him.

And Exodus 33:17-23
And the Lord said unto Moses, I will do this thing also that thou hast spoken: for thou hast found grace in my sight, and I know

thee by name. And he said, I beseech thee, shew me thy glory. And he said, I will make all my goodness pass before thee, and I will proclaim the name of the Lord before thee; and will be gracious to whom I will be gracious, and will shew mercy on those I will shew mercy. **And he said, thou canst not see my face: for there shall no man see me, and live.** And the Lord said, Behold, there is a place by me, and thou shalt stand upon a rock: And it shall come to pass, while my glory passeth by, that I will put thee in a cleft of the rock, and will cover thee with my hand while I pass by: And I will take away mine hand, and thou shalt see my back parts: **but my face shall not be seen.**

With Genesis 32:30
And Jacob called the name of the place Peniel: **For I have seen God face to face and my life is preserved.**

And Genesis 18:1
And the Lord appeared unto him in the plains of Mamre: and he sat in the tent door in the heat of the day.

According to John 1:18, the Holy Spirit's divinely inspired scripture clearly states that no man hath seen God at any time. This is written in the New Testament, which everyone knows was written after the Old Testament. Yet even back in the Old Testament book of Exodus 33:17-23, the Holy Spirit's divinely inspired scripture clearly states God's own words as saying, "Thou canst not see my face: for there shall no man see me, and live." However, in Genesis 32:30 Jacob is saying, "…I have seen God face to face, and my life is preserved." And in Genesis 18:1, it is written that, "…And the Lord appeared unto him…" This was in reference to Abraham. I'm not a person who can say what God can or cannot do. God can suspend his own rules if God wants to. But God is not the author of confusion. God knows how fragile we humans are, so I don't believe God would divinely inspire the Holy Spirit to cause the authors of the Holy Bible to be writing down confusing and contradictory statements in different places of the Bible.

I've confronted a few ministers and priests about some of these contradictions that I have found in the Bible. They would tell me off the top of their heads that when Abraham said that the Lord appeared to him, Abraham meant an angel appeared to him. That is the way clergymen would brush me off. Well I'm saying that is not good enough. God didn't have a problem divinely inspiring "angel" to be written down when he meant "angel" and "Lord" to be written down when he meant himself. Examples of this are in Psalms 34:7 and Luke 1:11.

<u>Psalm 34:7</u>
The angel of the Lord encampeth round about them that fear him, and delivereth them.

<u>Luke 1:11</u>
And there appeared unto him **an angel of the Lord** standing on the right side of the altar of incense.

God is not the author of confusion, and God wouldn't cause his Holy Spirit's divine inspiration to record his words in a contradictory way in the Holy Bible. All four of the above scripture references cannot be divinely inspired because they contradict each other. Either John 1:18 and Exodus 33:17-23, or Genesis 32:30 and Genesis 18:1 are incorrect. One or the other have been tampered with and interpolated. It is glaringly apparent that both sets of scripture references can't be accurate. Something is definitely wrong. Something is flawed, and I don't believe the mistake is on God. I believe there are flaws, errors, and interpolations in today's Bible. Any flaws, errors, and interpolations in today's Bible can be directly linked to man tampering with God's original divinely inspired Holy Bible. After you have examined the above scripture references in your own Bible to verify the scripture references that I have pointed out, let's go on to look at some more confusing and contradictory scripture references that I have a problem with in today's Bible.

Compare John 8:14

Jesus answered and said unto them, **Though I bear record of myself, yet my record is true:** for I know whence I came, and whither I go; but you cannot tell whence I come, and whither I go.

With John 5:30-31

I can of mine own self do nothing: as I hear, I judge: and my judgment is just; because I seek not mine own will, but the will of the Father which hath sent me. **If I bear witness of myself, my witness is not true.**

Here again are statements that contradict each other. I ask you; would God's Holy Spirit divinely inspire such confusing statements to be written down in the Holy Bible for his lambs and beloved sheep to read? I seriously doubt it. Let's read further and see some more flaws and errors I have discovered in today's Bible.

Chapter 16 - Who was the Son the King of Hamath Sent to David

<u>Compare 2 Samuel 8:5-11</u>
And when the Syrians of Damascus came to succor Hadadezer king of Zobah, David slew of the Syrians two and twenty thousand men. Then David put garrisons in Syria of Damascus: and the Syrians became servants to David, and brought gifts. And the Lord preserved David whithersoever he went. And David took the shields of gold that were on the servants of Hadadezer, and brought them to Jerusalem. And from **Betah**, and from **Berothai**, cities of Hadadezer, king David took exceeding much brass. When **Toi** king of Hamath heard that David had smitten all the hosts of Hadadezer, Then **Toi** sent **Joram** his son unto king David, to salute him, and to bless him, because he had fought against Hadadezer, and smitten him: for Hadadezer had wars with **Toi**. And **Joram** brought with him vessels of silver, and vessels of gold, and vessels of brass.

Which also king David did dedicate unto the Lord, with the silver and gold that he had dedicated of all nations which he subdued.

<u>With 1 Chronicles 18:5-11</u>

And when the Syrians of Damascus came to help Hadarezer king of Zobah, David slew of the Syrians two and twenty thousand men. Then David put garrisons in Syriadamascus; and the Syrians became David's servants, and brought gifts. Thus the Lord preserved David withersoever he went. And David took the shields of gold that were on the servants of Hadarezer, and brought them to Jerusalem. Likewise from **Tibhath**, and from **Chun**, cities of Hadarezer, brought David very much brass, wherewith Solomon made the brassen sea, and the pillars, and the vessels of brass. Now when **Tou** king of Hamath heard how David had smitten all the host of Hadarezer king of Zobah; He sent **Hadoram** his son to king David, to enquire of his welfare, and to congratulate him, because he had fought against Hadarezer, and smitten him; (for Hadarezer had war with **Tou**;) and with him all manner of vessels of gold and silver and brass. Them also king David dedicated unto the Lord, with the silver and the gold that he brought from all these nations; from Edom, and from Moab, and from the children of Ammon, and from the Philistines, and from Amalek.

BOTH OF THE above scripture reference in 2 Samuel 8:5-11 and 1 Chronicles 18:5-11 have an account of the same historical event of how David slew 22,000 Syrians in a battle, down to where David dedicated unto the Lord all the silver, gold, and brass that were taken as spoil from David's enemies. However, there are flaws in these two scripture references which I highlighted in bold so that you can easily see and compare between the two. The first flaw is about the cities of Hadarezer where David got a lot of brass from as the spoils of war. Which two cities were they? Were they Betah and Berothal; as it states in the 2 Samuel 8:5-11 account? Or were the cities Tibhath and Chun, as it states in the 1 Chronicles 18:5-11 account? Also notice that I highlighted in bold the name of the king of Hamath. It is Toi in the 2 Samuel account and Tou in the 1 Chronicles account. I suspect this may be a variation of the spelling of the king's name and not two different kings. But which son did the king of Hamath actually send to David? Was it the son Joram who was sent to David as it states in the 2 Samuel chapter 8 account? Or was it Hadoram as it states in the 1 Chronicles chapter 18 account? Here again is more proof that today's Bible has flaws and errors in it. I'm not forgetting all the times I've heard the clergy preach from the pulpit that if there is one mistake in the Bible, you can't believe any of it. I say that God's Holy Spirit can divinely inspire what he wants written down to be consistent in the various parts of the Bible. The clergy worldwide have been preaching from the pulpit that the Bible is the flawless Holy Spirit inspired WORD OF GOD. They have been telling us sheep that the Bible is God's Word and God's Word is infallible. These types of comments are routinely stated from the pulpits around the world to us sheep. But through my extensive study and research, I have discovered much more than one jot or tittle being out of place in today's Bible, which leads me to believe that the Bible we have today has been interpolated by men who were not led by God's Holy Spirit. Let's read on in my book as I point out more flaws and errors that I have discovered and have a problem with in today's Bible.

Chapter 17 - How Many Men Did David's Chief Captain Slay at One Time

<u>Compare 2 Samuel 23:8-9</u>

These be the names of the mighty men whom David had: **The Tachmonite that sat in the seat, chief among the captains; the same was Adino the Ezinite: he lift up his spear against <u>eight hundred</u> whom he slew at one time.** And after him was Eleazar the son of Dodo the Ahohite, one of the three mighty men with David, where they defied the Philistines that were there gathered together to battle, and the men of Israel were gone away:

<u>With 1 Chronicles 11:10-13</u>

These also are the chief of the mighty men whom David had, who strengthened themselves with him in his kingdom, and with all Israel, to make him king, according to the word of the Lord concerning Israel. And this is the number of the mighty men whom David had: **Jashobeam, an Hachmonite, the chief of the captains: he lifted up his spear against <u>three hundred</u> slain by him at one time.** And after him was Eleazar the son of Dodo, the Ahohite, who was one of the three mighties. He was with David at Pasdammim, and there the Philistines were gathered together to battle, where was a parcel of ground full of barley; and the people fled from before the Philistines.

DON'T FORGET TO look each and every one of these scripture references up in your own Bible to verify the facts that I am pointing out to you about the flaws and errors in today's Bible. Don't take my word for it. Don't let any man come between you and God. Not me, nor any clergy in the pulpit that tells you the Bible is the infallible, unaltered, unerring WORD OF GOD. It is not, and I am proving it to you.

Now let's examine the flaws between 2 Samuel 23:8-9 and 1 Chronicles 11:10-13. These two scripture references speak of the same account concerning the battle of the mighty men of David, down to Dodo the Ahohite, who was one of the three mighty men with David when the Philistines gathered together to do battle. If you closely examine the parts that I highlighted in bold in 2 Samuel 23:8-9 and in 1 Chronicles 11:10-13, you will see flaws and errors in their accuracy. Who was the chief among the captains? Was it the Tachmonite as it states in 2 Samuel? Or was it Hashobeam the Hachmonite as it states in 1 Chronicles? And how many men were slain at one time? Was it eight hundred as it says in 2 Samuel? Or was it three hundred as it says in 1 Chronicles? God is not the author of confusion. God would not cause the Holy Spirit to divinely inspire one set of facts to be written down in one place in the Bible about a certain battle, and then cause the facts to be flawed in another part of the Bible. God knows the beginning from the end and doesn't make any mistakes. This is just more proof that I have to offer for you to look at to decide if the Bible has been interpolated or not. Read on and I will show you more proof that what we've been told about the Holy Bible is a lie.

Chapter 18 - Was God or Satan Angry with Israel

Compare 2 Samuel 24:1

And again **the anger of the Lord was angered against Israel, and he moved David against them to say, Go, number Israel and Judah.**

With 1 Chronicles 21:1-2

And Satan stood up against Israel, and provoked David to number Israel. And David said to Joab and to the rulers of the people, Go, number Israel from BeerSheba even to Dan; and bring the number to me that I may know it.

HERE WE HAVE an account of the time that David decided to number Israel. But who exactly was angry against Israel? Was it the Lord as it states in the 2 Samuel 24:1 account? Or was it Satan, as it states in the 1 Chronicles 21:1-2 account? They both can't be right. Here again I prove that there are flaws and inaccuracies in the Bible, which are not only errors, but are quite confusing to today's Christians. Since God is not the author of confusion, then who caused these flaws? It was men who were not divinely inspired by God who made interpolations in the original divinely inspired Word of God. It was the first Nicene Council of 325 A.D.

that took it upon themselves to decide (for God?) which books of the Bible were "in" and which books were "out." And it was the subsequent councils, kings, and the various religious bodies that revised, translated, and interpolated the Holy Bible. These and the decisions of the various ecclesiastical councils over a thousand years ago caused these flaws and errors that we have in today's Bible which I have discovered through my extensive research and am pointing out to you sincere, God loving, lambs of God. Read my book with an open mind and look up all the scripture references in your own Bible, then after prayer and meditation with God, decide if you believe today's Bible is flawed and has been interpolated or not.

Chapter 19 - Is This Plagiarism

IN THE FOLLOWING I will quote chapter 19 from 2 Kings and then chapter 37 from the book of Isaiah. Each chapter is rather long, slightly less than 40 verses. But bear with me while you read these two chapters and compare them against each other. Of course you should also look them up in your own Bible as well to make sure I have quoted them accurately. When you compare the chapters of the two different books of the Bible, see if it doesn't look like one author plagiarized the other author word for word. Read on, look it up in your own Bible, and compare these two entire chapters out of the Bible for plagiarism as the later writer copies the earlier writer.

Compare 2 Kings 19
And it came to pass, when king Hezekiah heard it, that he rent his clothes, and covered himself with sackcloth, and went into the house of the Lord. And he sent Eliakim, which was over the household, and Shebna the scribe, and the elders of the priests, covered with sackcloth, to Isaiah the prophet the son of Amoz. And they said unto him, Thus saith Hezekiah, This day is a day of trouble, and of rebuke, and blasphemy: for the children are come to the birth, and there is not strength to bring forth. It may be the Lord thy God will hear all the words of Rabshakeh, whom the

king of Assyria his master hath sent to reproach the living God; and will reprove the words which the Lord thy God hath heard: wherefore lift up thy prayer for the remnant that are left. So the servants of king Hezekiah came to Isaiah. And Isaiah said unto them, Thus shall ye say to your master, Thus saith the Lord, Be not afraid of the words which thou hast heard, with which the servants of the king of Assyria have blasphemed me. Behold, I will sent a blast upon him, and he shall hear a rumour, and shall return to his own land; and I will cause him to fall by the sword in his own land.

So Rabshakeh returned, and found the king of Assyria warring against Libnah: for he had heard that he was departed from Lachish. And when he heard say of Tirhakah king of Ethopia, Behold, he is come out to fight against thee: he sent messengers again unto Hezekiah, saying, Thus shall ye speak to Hezekiah king of Judah, saying, Let not thy God in whom thou trustest deceive thee, saying, Jerusalem shall not be delivered into the hand of the king of Assyria. Behold, thou hast heard what the kings of Assyria have done to all lands, by destroying them utterly: and shalt thou be delivered? Have the gods of the nations delivered them which my fathers have destroyed; as Gozan, and Haran, and Rezeph, and the children of Eden which were in Thelasar? Where is the king of Hamath, and the king of Arpad, and the king of the city of Sepharvaim, of Hena, and Ivah? And Hezekiah received the letter of the hand the messengers, and read it: and Hezekiah went up into the house of the Lord, and spread it before the Lord. And Hezekiah prayed before the Lord, and said, O Lord God of Israel, which dwellest between the cherubims, thou art the God; even thou alone, of all the kingdoms of the earth; thou hast made heaven and earth. Lord, bow down thine ear, and hear; open, Lord, thine eyes, and see: and hear the words of Sennacherib, which hath sent him to reproach the living God. Of a truth, Lord, the kings of Assyria have destroyed the nations and their lands. And have cast their gods into the fire: for they were no gods, but the work of men's hands, wood and stone: therefore they have destroyed them. Now therefore, O Lord our God, I beseech thee, save thou us out of his hand, that all the kingdoms of the earth may know that thou art the Lord God, even thou only. Then Isaiah the son of Amoz sent to Hezekiah, saying, Thus saith the Lord God of Israel, That which thou hast prayed to me against Sennacherib king of Assyria I have heard. This is the word that the Lord hath spoken concerning him; The virgin the daughter of Zion hath despised thee, and laughed thee to scorn; the daughter of Jerusalem hath shaken her head at thee. Whom hast thou reproached and blasphemed? and against whom hast thou exalted thy voice, and lifted up thine eyes on high? even against the Holy One of Israel. By the messengers thou has reproached the Lord, and hast said, With the multitude of my chariots I am come up to the height of the mountains, to the sides of Lebanon, and will cut down the tall cedar trees thereof, and the choice fir trees thereof: and I will enter into the lodgings of his borders, and into the forest of his Carmel. I have digged and drunk strange waters, and with the sole of my feet have I dried up all the rivers of besieged places. Hast thou not heard long ago how I have done it, and of ancient times that I have formed it? now have I brought it to pass, that thou shouldest be to lay waste fenced cities into ruinous heaps. Therefore their inhabitants were of small power, they were dismayed and confounded; they were as the grass of the field, and as the green herb, as the grass on the house tops, and as corn blasted before it be grown up. But I know thy abode, and thy going out, and thy coming in, and thy rage against me. Because thy rage against me and thy tumult is come up into mine ears, therefore I will put my hook in thy nose, and my bridle in thy lips, and I will turn thee back by the way by which thou camest. And this shall be a sign unto thee, Ye shall eat this year such things as grow of themselves, and in the second year that which springeth of the same; and in the third year sow ye, and reap, and plant vineyards, and eat the fruits thereof. And the remnant that is escaped of the house of Judah shall yet again take root downward, and bear fruit upward. For out of Jerusalem shall go forth a remnant, and they that escape out of mount Zion: the zeal of the Lord of hosts shall do this.

Therefore thus saith the Lord concerning the king of Assyria, He shall not come into this city, nor shoot an arrow there, nor come before it with shield, nor cast a bank against it. By the way that he came, by the same shall he return, and shall not come into this city, saith the Lord. For I will defend this city, to save it, for mine own sake, and for my servant David's sake. And it came to pass that night, that the angel of the Lord went out, and smote in the camp of the Assyrians an hundred fourscore and five thousand: and when they arose early in the morning, behold, they were all dead corpses. So Sennacherib king of Assyria departed, and went and returned, and dwelt at Nineveh. And it came to pass, as he was worshipping in the house of Nisroch his god, that Adrammelech and Sharezer his sons smote him with the sword: and they escaped unto the land of Armenia. And Esarhaddon his son reigned in his stead.

<u>With Isaiah 37</u>
And it came to pass, when king Hezekiah heard it, that he rent his clothes, and covered himself with sackcloth, and went into the house of the Lord. And he sent Eliakim, who was over the household, and Shebna the scribe, and the elders of the priests covered with sackcloth, unto Isaiah the prophet the son of Amoz. And they said unto him, Thus saith Hezekiah, This day is a day of trouble, and of rebuke, and of blasphemy: for the children are come to the birth, and there is not strength to bring forth. It may be the Lord thy God will hear the words of Rabshakeh, whom the king of Assyria his master hath sent to reproach the living God, and will reprove the words which the Lord thy God hath heard: wherefore lift up thy prayer for the remnant that is left. So the servants of the king Hezekiah came to Isaiah. And Isaiah said unto them, Thus shall ye say unto your master, Thus saith the Lord, Be not afraid of the words that thou hast heard, wherewith

the servants of the king of Assyria have blasphemed me. Behold, I will send a blast upon him, and he shall hear a rumour, and return to his own land; and I will cause him to fall by the sword in his own land. So Rabshakeh returned, and found the king of Assyria warring against Libnah: for he had heard that he was departed from Lachish. And he heard say concerning Tirhakah king of Ethopia, He is come forth to make war with thee. And when he heard it, he sent messengers to Hezekiah, saying, Thus shall ye speak to Hezekiah king of Judah, saying, Let not thy God, in whom thou trustest, deceive thee, saying, Jerusalem shall not be given into the hand of the king of Assyria. Behold, thou hast heard what the kings of Assyria have done to all lands by destroying them utterly; and shalt thou be delivered? Have the gods of the nations delivered them which my fathers have destroyed, as Gozan, and Haran, and Rezeph, and the children of Eden which were in Telassar? Where is the king of Hamath, and the king of Arphad, and the king of the city of Sepharvaim, Hena, and Ivah? And Hezekiah received the letter from the hand of the messengers, and read it: and Hezekiah went up unto the house of the Lord, and spread it before the Lord. And Hezekiah prayed unto the Lord, saying, O Lord of hosts, God of Israel, that dwellest between the cherubims, that art the God, even thou alone, of all the kingdoms of the earth: thou hast made heaven and earth. Incline thine ear, O Lord, and hear: open thine eyes, O Lord, and see: and hear all the words of Sennacherib, which hath sent to reproach the living God. Of a truth, Lord, the kings of Assyria have laid waste all the nations, and their countries. And have cast their gods into the fire: for they were no gods, but the work of men's hands, wood and stone: therefore they have destroyed them.

Now therefore, O Lord our God, save us from his hand, that all the kingdoms of the earth may know that thou art the Lord, even thou only. Then Isaiah the son of Amoz sent unto Hezekiah, saying, Thus saith the Lord God of Israel, Whereas thou hast prayed to me against Sennacherib king of Assyria: This is the word which the Lord hath spoken concerning him; The virgin, the daughter of Zion, hath despised thee, and laughed thee to scorn; the daughter of Jerusalem hath shown her head at thee. Whom hast thou reproached and blasphemed? and against whom hast thou exalted thy voice, and lifted up thine eyes on high? even against the Holy One of Israel. By thy servants hast thou reproached the Lord, and hast said, By the multitude of my chariots am I come up to the height of the mountains, to the sides of Lebanon; and I will cut down the tall cedars thereof, and the choice fir trees thereof: and I will enter into the height of his border, and the forest of his Carmel. I have digged, and drunk water; and with the sole of my feet have I dried up all the rivers of the besieged places. Hast thou not heard long ago, how I have done it; and of ancient times, that I have formed it? now I have brought it to pass, that thou shouldest be to lay waste defenced cities into ruinous heaps. Therefore their inhabitants were of small power, they were dismayed and confounded: they were as the grass of the field, and as the green herb, as the grass on the housetops, and as corn blasted before it be grown up. But I know thy abode, and thy going out, and thy coming in, and thy rage against me. Because thy rage against me, and thy tumult, is come up into mine ears, therefore will I put my hook in thy nose, and my bridle in thy lips, and I will turn thee back by the way by which thou camest. And this shall be a sign unto thee, Ye shall eat this year such as groweth of itself; and the second year that which springeth of the same: and in the third year sow ye, and reap, and plant vineyards, and eat the fruit thereof. And the remnant that is escaped of the house of Judah shall again take root downward, and bear fruit upward: For out of Jerusalem shall go forth a remnant, and they that escape out of mount Zion: the zeal of the Lord of hosts shall do this. Therefore thus saith the Lord concerning the king of Assyria, He shall not come into this city, nor shoot an arrow there, nor come before it with shields, nor cast a bank against it. By the way that he came, by the same shall he return, and shall not come into this city, saith the Lord. For I will defend this city to save it for mine own sake, and for my servant David's sake. Then the angel of the Lord went forth and smote in the camp of the Assyrians a hundred and fourscore and five thousand: and when they arose early in the morning, behold, they were all dead corpses. So Sennacherib king of Assyria departed, and went and returned, and dwelt at Nineveh. And it came to pass, as he was worshipping in the house of Nisroch his god, that Adramcnelech and Sharezer his sons smote him with the sword; and they escaped into the land of Armenia: and Esarhaddon his son reigned in his stead.

After having closely examined the above chapter 19 of 2 Kings and chapter 37 of Isaiah, (while also checking it in your own Bible to verify that I quoted the two chapters properly), it appears that one author plagiarized the other author word for word in these two chapters. How can this be? God is not the author of confusion. God wouldn't "forget" that he already divinely inspired one author to write the words of this chapter down in his Holy Bible. Therefore I have given you another proof that today's Bible has been interpolated.

Chapter 20 - Are Our Ministers Lying to Us by Omission

IN THE FOLLOWING 8 scripture references that I will quote from the Bible, I find no flaws or errors in the text. However, from all the preaching and sermons I've heard from ministers, priests, and televangelists, you would think that God never divinely inspired these scriptures to be written down. When you read the following 8 scripture references, and after checking in your own Bible to be sure that I quoted them correctly, compare it with the homemade words that have been coming at you from the pulpit of your place of worship, and decide if your clergy is telling it to you straight or not. You will better understand the point I am making after you read and meditate on these scripture references.

Exodus 4:10-12
And Moses said unto the Lord, O my Lord, I am not eloquent, neither heretofore, nor since thou hast spoken unto thy servant: but I am slow of speech, and of a slow tongue. **And the Lord said unto him, Who hath made man's mouth? or who maketh the dumb, or deaf, or the seeing, or the blind? have not I the Lord?** Now therefore go, and I will be with thy mouth, and teach thee what thou shalt say.

Isaiah 45:5-8
I am the Lord, and there is none else, there is no God beside me: I girded thee, though thou has not known me: That they may know from the rising of the sun, and from the west, that there is none beside me. I am the Lord, and there is none else. **I form the light, and create darkness: I make peace, and create evil: I the Lord do all these things.** Drop down, ye heavens, from above and let the skies pour down righteousness: let the earth open, and let them bring forth salvation, and let righteousness spring up together; I the Lord have created it.

Micah 1:12
For the inhabitant of Maroth waited carefully for good: **but evil came down from the Lord unto the gate of Jerusalem.**

Numbers 14:11-12
And the Lord said unto Moses, How long will this people provoke me? and how long will it be ere they believe me, for all the signs which I have shewed among them? **I will smite them with the pestilence,** and disinherit them, and will make of thee a greater nation and mightier than they.

1 Samuel 16:14
But the Spirit of the Lord departed from Saul, **and an evil spirit from the Lord troubled him.**

Romans 9:14-26
What shall we say then? Is there unrighteousness with God? God forbid. For he saith to Moses, I will have mercy on whom I will have mercy, and I will have compassion on whom I will have compassion. So then it is not of him that willeth, nor of him that runneth, but of God that sheweth mercy. For the scripture saith unto Pharaoh, Even for this same purpose have I raised thee up, that I might shew my power in thee, and that my name might be declared throughout all the earth. **Therefore hath he mercy on whom he will have mercy, and whom he will he hardeneth.**

Thou wilt say then unto me, Why doth he yet find fault? For who hath resisted his will? Nay but, O man, who art thou that repliest against God? Shall the thing formed say to him that formed it, Why hast thou made me thus?

Hath not the potter power over the clay, of the same lump to make one vessel unto honour, and another unto dishonour? What if God, willing to shew his wrath, and to make his power known, endured with much longsuffering the vessels of wrath fitted to destruction: And that he might make known the riches of his glory on the vessels of mercy, which he had afore prepared unto glory, Even us, whom he hath called, not of the Jews only, but also of the Gentiles? As he saith also in Osee, I will call them my people, which were not my people; and her beloved, which was not beloved. And it shall come to pass, that in the place where it was said unto them, Ye are not my people; there shall they be called the children of the living God.

Exodus 14:1-18
And the Lord spake unto Moses, saying. Speak unto the children of Israel, that they turn and encamp before Pihahiroth, between Migdol and the sea, over against Baalzephon: before it shall ye encamp by the sea. For Pharaoh will say of the children of Israel, They are entangled in the land, the wilderness hath shut them in. **And I will harden Pharaoh's heart, that he shall follow after them;** and I will be honored upon Pharaoh, and upon all his host; that the Egyptians may know that I am the Lord, And they did so. And it was told the king of Egypt that the people fled: and the heart of Pharaoh and of his servants was turned against the people, and they said, Why have we done this, that we have let Israel go from serving us? And he made ready his chariot, and took his people with him: And he took six hundred chosen chariots, and all the chariots of Egypt, and captains over every one of them. **And the Lord hardened the heart of Pharaoh king of Egypt, and he pursued after the children of Israel:** and the children of Israel went out with an high hand. But the Egyptians

pursued after them, all the horses and chariots of Pharaoh, and his horsemen, and his army, and overtook them encamping by the sea, beside Pihahiroth, before Baalzephon. And when Pharaoh drew nigh, the children of Israel lifted up their eyes, and, behold, the Egyptians marched after them; and they were sore afraid: and the children of Israel cried out unto the Lord. And they said unto Moses, Because there were no graves in Egypt, hast thou taken us away to die in the wilderness? wherefore hast thou dealt thus with us, to carry us forth out of Egypt? Is not this the word that we did tell thee in Egypt, saying, Let us alone, that we may serve the Egyptians? For it had been better for us to serve the Egyptians, than that we should die in the wilderness. And Moses said unto the people, Fear ye not, stand still, and see the salvation of the Lord, which he will shew to you today: for the Egyptians whom ye have seen today, ye shall see them again no more for ever. The Lord shall fight for you, and ye shall hold your peace. And the Lord said unto Moses, Wherefore criest thou unto me? speak unto the children of Israel, that they go forward: But lift thou up thy rod, and stretch out thine hand over the sea, and divide it: and the children of Israel shall go on dry ground through the midst of the sea. **And I, behold, I will harden the hearts of the Egyptians, and they shall follow them:** and I will get me honor upon Pharaoh, and upon all his host, upon his chariots, and upon his horsemen. And the Egyptians shall know that I am the Lord, when I have gotten me honour upon Pharaoh, upon his chariots, and upon his horsemen.

Exodus 10:1-29
And the Lord said unto Moses, Go in unto Pharaoh: for I have hardened his heart, and the heart of his servants, that I might shew these my signs before him: And that thou mayest tell in the ears of thy son, and of thy son's son, what things I have wrought in Egypt, and my signs which I have done among them; that ye may know how that I am the Lord. And Moses and Aaron came in unto Pharaoh, and said unto him, Thus saith the Lord God of

the Hebrews, How long wilt thou refuse to humble thyself before me? let my people go, that they may serve me. Else, if thou refuse to let my people go, behold, tomorrow will I bring the locusts into thy coast: And they shall cover the face of the earth, that one cannot be able to see the earth: and they shall eat the residue of that which is escaped, which remaineth unto you from the hail, and shall eat every tree which groweth for you out of the field: And they shall fill thy houses, and the houses of all thy servants, and the houses of all the Egyptians; which neither thy fathers, nor thy fathers' fathers have seen, since the day that they were upon the earth unto this day. And he turned himself, and went out from Pharaoh. And Pharaoh's servants said unto him, How long shall this man be a snare unto us? let the men go, that they may serve the Lord their God: knowest thou not yet that Egypt is destroyed? And Moses and Aaron were brought again unto Pharaoh: and he said unto them, Go, serve the Lord your God: but who are they that shall go? And Moses said, We will go with our young and with our old, with our sons and with our daughters, with our flocks and with our herds will we go; for we must hold a feast unto the Lord. And he said unto them, Let the Lord be so with you, as I will let you go, and your little ones: look to it; for evil is before you. Not so: go now ye that are men, and serve the Lord; for that ye did desire. And they were driven out from Pharaoh's presence. And the Lord said unto Moses, Stretch out thine hand over the land of Egypt for the locusts, that they may come upon the land of Egypt, and eat every herb of the land, even all that the hail hath left. And Moses stretched forth his rod over the land of Egypt, and the Lord brought an east wind upon the land all that day, and all that night; and when it was morning, the east wind brought the locusts. And the locusts went up over all the land of Egypt, and rested in all the coasts of Egypt: very grievous were they; before them there were no such locusts as they, neither after them shall be such. For they covered the face of the whole earth, so that the land was darkened; and they did eat every herb of the land, and all the fruit of the trees which the hail had left: and there remained not any green thing in the trees, or in the herbs of the field, through all the land of Egypt. Then Pharaoh called for Moses and Aaron in haste; and he said, I have sinned against the Lord your God, and against you. Now therefore forgive, I pray thee, my sin only this once, and entreat the Lord your God, that he may take away from me this death only. And he went out from Pharaoh, and entreated the Lord. And the Lord turned a mighty strong west wind, which took away the locusts, and cast them into the Red sea; there remained not one locust in all the coasts of Egypt. **But the Lord hardened Pharaoh' s heart, so that he would not let the children of Israel go.** And the Lord said unto Moses, Stretch out thine hand toward heaven, that there may be darkness over the land of Egypt, even darkness which may be felt. And Moses stretched forth his hand toward heaven; and there was a thick darkness in all the land of Egypt three days: They saw not one another, neither rose any from his place for three days: but all the children of Israel had light in their dwellings. And Pharaoh called unto Moses, and said, Go ye, serve the Lord; only let your flocks and your herds be stayed: let your little ones also go with you.

And Moses said, Thou must give us also sacrifices and burnt offerings, that we may sacrifice unto the Lord our God. Our cattle also shall go with us; there shall not an hoof be left behind; for thereof must we take to serve the Lord our God; and we know not with what we must serve the Lord, until we come thither. **But the Lord hardened Pharaoh's heart, and he would not let them go.** And Pharaoh said unto him, Get thee from me, take heed to thyself, see my face no more; for in that day thou seest my face thou shalt die. And Moses said, Thou hast spoken well, I will see thy face again no more.

If you folks are like me, from the assortment of ministers, priests, and televangelists that I've been listening to and getting instruction from, I haven't heard the clergy preach about God in the way that God's word is quoted in the above 8 scriptures. But this is God's word that he divinely inspired to have written down. In Exodus 10:1-29 we hear the Lord stating directly to Moses that the Lord is the one who hardened Pharaoh's heart. In Exodus 14:1-18 we again see that the Lord God Almighty takes credit for hardening Pharaoh's heart as well as the heart of the Egyptians. In Numbers 14:11-12 we see the Lord telling Moses that he will smite people with pestilence. In Micah 1:12 we see that evil came down from the Lord to those in Jerusalem. In Isaiah 45:5-8 we see God saying he creates evil. In Exodus 4:10-12 we see God telling Moses that it is the Lord who makes the deaf unhearing and the dumb unspeaking. And in Romans 9:14-26 we see that God will have mercy on whom he will have mercy, and he will harden whom he will harden, as that is God's prerogative. Is this what you have been hearing from the clergy in the pulpit? It's not what I have been hearing. What I hear, and what I'm guessing that most of you have been hearing, is only about where in John 10:10 it says that, the thief (meaning Satan) comes not, but for to steal, and to kill, and to destroy. The televangelists, ministers, and priests that I listen to are stuck on this one point and don't go on to tell you about the other 8 scriptures that I have pointed out to you here about God's hand in events. I debated with myself if I should even include this part in my book, since this is not directly about flaws and errors in the Bible. I decided to include it because I sincerely care about the lambs of God who fill up the church pews and are not hearing the whole picture. Hosea 4:6a says, "My people are destroyed for lack of knowledge..." And if the rest of the rank and file Christians are only hearing one side of the Bible from their clergy, I wanted to offer them "the rest of the story," the rest that they may not be hearing in their home church. I'm guessing their minister is manipulating the lambs of God by only giving them a slanted picture of God and the Bible, instead of giving them the whole picture. Just because we have started the second millennium, God hasn't changed since before he created the solar system and the earth and put us in the earth. This can be evidenced by God's own word about himself in

Malachi 3:6a where he says, "For I am the Lord, I change not..." In Isaiah 44:6b he is quoted as saying, "...I am the first, and I am the last; and beside me there is no God." And in Hebrews 13:8 it says, "Jesus Christ the same yesterday, and to day, and for ever." Therefore we have God's own words telling us that there is only one God and he is always the same. So why are we routinely given such a watered down version from the pulpit of God, evil, and the source of deafness, dumbness, and pestilence? I'm guessing it's because they either aren't anointed by God to speak for him, and/ or they are just intent on furthering their own agenda, without true regard for the lambs of God. I sincerely care for the lambs of God, and I want them/us all to get the entire picture of God and the Bible. That is why I am writing this book.

I will never name any one minister, priest, or televangelist. My book is not to point out any individual(s) specifically. There are some good ministers out there who preach all of the facts about the Bible that I am pointing out to you in my book. They know who they are. For the ministers, priests, and televangelists who are informing their lambs in the pews as I am informing them in my book, the shoe doesn't fit them. And if the shoe doesn't fit, then don't wear it. It's as simple as that. Even though my book is primarily directed at the non-clergy (laity), I will briefly say to the ministers, priests, and televangelists in the pulpit that are selectively omitting the scripture references that I am pointing out in my book, regarding the flaws, errors, and interpolations, stop withholding information from the laity. You are a Bible College-graduated, trained professional and you know better. Stop it! Stop trying to produce "cookie cutter" Christians, where all the lambs of God are alike because they all have been kept in the dark about the interpolations in today's Bible.

I will remind the laity that there is only one God and he hasn't changed. It is up to you to do as we are instructed in 2 Timothy 2:15, "study to shew thyself approved unto God, a workman that needeth not to be ashamed, rightly dividing the word of truth."

So you need to look into the Bible for yourself so you will know whether what the clergy is telling you from the pulpit is the whole truth or not. You need to look up the scripture references that I am pointing out to you about the flaws and errors in the Bible for yourself to see if they are really there as I have quoted them in my book. I'm only human, and as well intentioned as I am, I sometimes do make inadvertent mistakes. Then pray and meditate with God about it. Invite God and his Holy Spirit to minister to your own spirit in helping you decide if today's Bible has been interpolated. By praying, and inviting God's Holy Spirit to merge with your own human spirit, you are following the scripture of John 16:13a where it says, "Howbeit when he, the Spirit of truth, is come, he will guide you into all truth..." We need to learn to look things up and think for ourselves through God's direction. In Matthew 24:24 it predicts (I'm paraphrasing) that there will arise false prophets who will deceive the very elect. Have you been deceived from the pulpits of your church by half truths? Have the clergy been deceived and that is why they only know to minister half truths to you? It is my opinion that Jesus did not bring "organized religion" to planet earth. Jesus brought Salvation. I believe humans invented organized religion by getting carried away with what Jesus said in Matthew 16:18 where he said, "And I say also unto thee, That thou art Peter, and upon this rock I will build my church: and the gates of hell shall not prevail against it." Jesus came to establish a Spiritual Kingdom as is reflected in Hebrews 5:8-9 where it says, "Though he were a Son, yet learned he obedience by the things which he suffered; And being made perfect, he became the author of eternal salvation unto all them that obey him." This is why I believe Jesus didn't come to earth to bring us organized religion. Jesus came to earth to bring Salvation to us. If the Bible wasn't interpolated, then we would have an excellent guidepost to follow. 2 Timothy 3:16 tells us that, "All scripture is given by inspiration of God, and is profitable for doctrine, for reproof, for correction, for instruction in righteousness." And 2 Peter 1:21 says, "For the prophecy came not in old time by the will of man: but holy men of God spake as they were moved by the Holy Ghost." This is why the lambs of God of today need to know that today's Bible has been interpolated. There are flaws and errors in today's Bible.

What I sincerely believe Jesus brought to planet earth is reflected in his words in John 17:1-26. Jesus's own words says it so much better than I can.

John 17:1-26

These words spake Jesus, and lifted up his eyes to heaven, and said, Father, the hour is come; glorify thy Son, that thy Son also may glorify thee: As thou hast given him power over all flesh, that he should give eternal life to as many as thou hast given him. And this is the life eternal, that they might know thee the only true God, and Jesus Christ, whom thou hast sent. I have glorified thee on the earth: I have finished the work which thou gavest me to do. And now, 0 Father, glorify thou me with thine own self with the glory which I had with thee before the world was. I have manifested thy name unto the men which thou gavest me out of the world: thine they were, and thou gavest them me; and they have kept thy word. Now they have known that all things whatsoever thou hast given me are of thee. For I have given unto them the words which thou gavest me; and they have received them, and have known surely that I came out from thee, and they have believed that thou didst send me. I pray for them: I pray not for the world, but for them which thou hast given me; for they are thine. And all mine are thine, and thine are mine; and I am glorified in them. And now I am no more in the world, but these are in the world, and I come to thee. Holy Father, keep through thine own name those whom thou has given me, **that they may be as one,** as we are. While I was with them in the world, I kept them in thy name: those that thou gavest me I have kept, and none of them is lost, but the son of perdition; that the scripture might be fulfilled. And now come I to thee; and these things I speak in the world, that they might have my joy fulfilled in themselves. I have given them thy word; and the world hath hated them, because they are not of the world, even as I am not of the world. I pray not that thou shouldest take them out of the world, but that thou shouldest keep them from the evil. They are not of the world, even as I am not of the world. Sanctify them through thy truth: thy word is truth. As thou hast sent me into the world, even so have I also sent them into the world. And for their sakes I sanctify myself, that they also might be sanctified through the truth. Neither pray I for these alone, but for them also which shall believe on me through their word; **That they all may be one; as thou, Father, art in me, and I in thee, that they also may be one in us:** that the world may believe that thou hast sent me. And the glory which thou gavest me I have given them; **that they may be one, even as we are one:** I in them, and thou in me, that they may be made perfect in one; and that the world may know that thou hast sent me, and hast loved them, as thou hast loved me. Father, I will that they also, whom thou hast given me, be with me where I am; that they may behold my glory, which thou hast given me: for thou lovedst me before the foundation of the world. O righteous Father, the world hath not known thee: but I have known thee, and these have known that thou hast sent me. And I have declared unto them thy name, and will declare it: that the love wherewith thou hast loved me may be in them, and I in them.

By paying especial attention to the parts that I have highlighted in bold, you can see in Jesus's own words that he wanted us all to be one with the heavenly Father. Jesus wanted us to be one with the one and only God Almighty. This is the same one and only God Almighty who says in Isaiah 45:5a, "I am the Lord, and there is none else, there is no God beside me..."

This is why I believe that Jesus did not bring "organized religion" to planet earth. Jesus came to planet earth to bring Salvation, and in his own words in John 17:11b, 21a, and 22b, Jesus said he wanted us to be one with God. I have a personal relationship with

God Almighty similar to Abraham's one on one relationship with God. One of the problems of organized religion is that when a person joins one religious denomination or sect, that person has tacitly put themselves above, and shut out, all other persons who do not believe the same way. Where is the unity in that? On the larger scale, that does more to divide than to unify. Yet Jesus' words in John 17 specifically say that he prays to the Father that we all may be one. It is definitely something for us all to think about and take to God in prayer. Do you have a personal one on one relationship with God? Or do you sit up under some person in the pulpit and believe whatever that person says you should believe? Okay, now I will get back to pointing out some of the flaws and errors I've found in today's interpolated Bible, and various problems with some things that I find in today's Bible.

Chapter 21 - Where did Water Come From

Genesis 1:1-13

In the beginning God created the heaven and the earth. And the earth was without form, and void; and darkness was upon the face of the deep. **And the Spirit of God moved upon the face of the waters.** And God said, Let there be light: and there was light. And God saw the light, that it was good: and God divided the light from the darkness. And God called the light Day, and the darkness he called Night. And the evening and the morning were the first day. **And God said, Let there be a firmament in the midst of the waters, and let it divide the waters from the waters. And God made the firmament, and divided the waters which were under the firmament from the waters which were above the firmament:** and it was so. And God called the firmament Heaven. And the evening and the morning were the second day. **And God said, Let the waters under the heaven be gathered together unto one place, and let the dry land appear: and it was so. And God called the dry land Earth; and the gathering together of the waters called he Seas:** and God saw that it was good. And God said, Let the earth bring forth grass, the herb yielding seed, and the fruit tree yielding fruit after his kind, whose seed is in itself, upon the earth: and it was so. And the earth brought forth grass, and herb yielding seed after his kind, and the tree yielding fruit, whose seed was in itself, after his kind: and God saw that it was good. And the evening and the morning were the third day.

THE ABOVE SCRIPTURE reference quotes the first three days of creation that the author of Genesis, Moses, is purported to have written down under God's Holy Spirit divine inspiration. At the same time we know, according to 1 Corinthians 14:33 that God is not the author of confusion. Therefore I don't believe God would divinely inspire confusion to be written down. Well then where did the water come from??? The entire first chapter of Genesis is devoted to documenting the creation of everything, but for some confusing reason the account omits the creation of the water. It is just one more flaw that I find in today's Bible that leads me to believe that today's Bible has been interpolated from when it was originally handed down from God to God's divinely inspired writers.

Chapter 22 - Dinosaurs, Fire Breathing Dragons and Giants

JUST FOR A point of curiosity and interest, I will quote the following scripture reference for you to look up and verify in your own Bible, even though there is no actual flaw that I can find. In Job, chapter 40 and 41, God mentions what I believe are reference to dinosaurs, where he mentions "behemoth" and "leviathan." And then God goes on to mention fire breathing dragons. Of course I believe God in faith, and even though I don't find an actual flaw in the following verses, I thought I would include them for you for their novelty value, as there possibly might be some of you who didn't know these references were in the Bible.

Job 40:15 through 41:25
Behold now <u>behemoth</u>, which I made with thee; he eateth grass as an ox. Lo now, his strength is in his loins, and his force is in the navel of his belly. He moveth his tail like a cedar: the sinews of his stones are wrapped together. His bones are as strong pieces of brass; his bones are like bars of iron. He is the chief of the ways of God: he that made him can make his sword to approach unto him. Surely the mountains bring him forth food, where all the beasts of the field play. He

lieth under the shady trees, in the cover of the reed, and fens. The shady trees cover him with their shadow; the willows of the brook compass him about. Behold, he drinketh up a river, and hasteth not: he trusteth that he can draw up Jordan into his mouth. He taketh it with his eyes: his nose pierceth through snares. **Canst thou draw out <u>leviathan</u> with an hook? or his tongue with a cord which thou lettest down?** Canst thou put an hook into his nose? or bore his jaw through with a thorn? Will he make many supplications unto thee? will he speak soft words unto thee? Will he make a covenant with thee? wilt thou take him for a servant for ever? Wilt thou play with him as with a bird? or wilt thou bind him for thy maidens? Shall the companions make a banquet of him? shall they part him among the merchants? Canst thou fill his skin with barbed irons? or his head with fish spears? Lay thine hand upon him, remember the battle, do no more. Behold, the hope of him is in vain: shall not one be cast down even at the sight of him? None is so fierce that dare stir him up: who then is able to stand before me? Who hath prevented me, that I should repay him? whatsoever is under the whole heaven is mine. I will not conceal his parts, nor his power, nor his comely proportion. Who can discover the face of his garment? or who can come to him with his double bridle? **Who can open the doors of his face? his teeth are terrible round about. His scales are his pride, shut up together as with a close seal. One is so near to another, that no air can come between them.** They are joined one to another, they stick together, that they cannot be sundered. By his sneezings a light doth shine, and his eyes are like the eyelids of the morning. **Out of his mouth go burning lamps, and sparks of fire leap out. Out of his nostrils goeth smoke, as out of a seething pot or caldron. His breath kindleth coals, and a flame goeth out of his mouth.** In his neck remaineth strength, and sorrow is turned into joy before him. The flakes of his flesh are joined together: they are firm in themselves; they cannot be moved. His heart is as firm as a stone; yea, as hard as a piece of the nether millstone. When he raiseth up himself, the mighty are afraid: by reason of breakings they purify themselves.

From God's descriptions in the above scripture references, especially the parts that I put in bold, God seems to be describing dinosaurs, as well as a fire breathing dragon. **Notice how God said he made the behemoth <u>with</u> thee? He didn't say he made them millions of years before man, but they were extinct by the time he made man to inhabit the earth.**

In Webster's Concise Family Dictionary, under behemoth, Webster claims the behemoth mentioned in Job 40:15 is probably in reference to a hippopotamus. I wholeheartedly disagree with that speculation, because if you go on to read Job 40:17, God says he (the behemoth) moves his tail like a cedar (tree). I can't see how the ancestor of today's hippopotamus was all that much different than today's hippo (a nearly tail-less hippopotamus, except for a palm-like stump) except possibly the great ancestor of today's hippo might have been larger. Yet I don't believe any 2000 year old hippos had a tail like a cedar tree, or any other tree-like tail for that matter. Therefore I believe the behemoth referred to in Job 40:15 sounds similar to one of the dinosaurs, like the herbivorous brontosaurus, or some such similar grass eating dinosaur having a tail like a cedar tree. The leviathan mentioned in Job 41:1 could be any large and formidable sea animal, possibly along the line of the Loch Ness Monster (although I believe whatever creature may have been [or is] in Loch Ness, it is not a "monster"). The verses in Job 41:14-16 describe a creature with terrible teeth and closely sealed scales. Of course God's description in Job 41:19-21 cannot be taken for anything other than a fire breathing dragon. Since God is not the author of confusion, I will accept that these descriptions that God is laying out for us here in Job are about the descendants of prehistoric dinosaurs, as well as a fire breathing dragon. I know that some evolutionary scientists have said that the dinosaurs died out long before homo sapiens appeared on planet earth. These words quoted as coming directly from God refute that evolutionary theory. Before I leave this rather lighthearted observation of scripture, I will include one more Bible scripture reference for you to think about containing mention of giants.

<u>Genesis 6:1-4</u>
And it came to pass, when men began to multiply on the face of the earth, and daughters were born unto them, That the sons of God saw the daughters of men that they were fair and they took them wives of all which they chose. And the Lord said, My spirit shall not always strive with man, for that he also is flesh: yet his days shall be an hundred and twenty years. **There were giants in the earth in those days;** and also after that, when the sons of God came in unto the daughters of men, and they bare children to them, the same became mighty men which were of old, men of renown.

The above scripture reference refers to giants, and the previous scripture reference that I pointed out to you referred to dinosaurs and a fire breathing dragon. In the parts of today's Bible where I don't find evidence that there are flaws, errors, and interpolations, I simply believe God's word in faith. Like I said earlier, I particularly enjoy the accounts in the Bible about dinosaurs, giants, and a fire breathing dragon, and I included it for those of you who might not have known these references were even in the Bible. After looking these up in your own Bible, you can draw your own conclusion about what God is describing in the above verses. I enjoyed lightening the mood with the above scripture references, but now I will get back to more serious problems that I have found with today's Bible, compared to what is being taught to us from the pulpit by the clergy.

Chapter 23 - Did God Give the Same Thing to Opposing Factions

Psalm 115:15-16
Ye are blessed of the Lord which made heaven and earth. The heaven, even the heavens, are the Lords: **but the earth hath he given to the children of men.**

ACCORDING TO WHAT has been taught to me from the pulpit by the clergy all of my life, (and I'm guessing the same thing has been taught to you too) before God even made man, he created the angels in heaven. Then after a time there was dissension in heaven against God and a war broke out with one-third of the rebellious angels, led by Lucifer. Lucifer, from then on called Satan, was cast down to earth with one-third of the angels that were with him in the war against God. Does this paraphrased overview of the story coincide with what your clergy have been telling you all of your life? The following scripture references talk about Lucifer and the angels that followed him in his rebellion against God, which gives credence to the teaching that the clergy has been giving us from the pulpit all of our lives.

Ezekiel 28:13-15
Thou has been in Eden the garden of God; every precious stone
was thy covering, the sardius, topaz, and the diamond, the beryl,
the onyx, and the jasper, the sapphire, the emerald, and the
carbuncle, and gold: the workmanship of thy tabrets and of thy
pipes was prepared in thee in the day that thou wast created. Thou
art the anointed cherub that covereth; and I have set thee so: thou
wast upon the holy mountain of God; thou hast walked up and
down in the midst of the stones of fire. **Thou wast perfect in thy
ways from the day that thou wast created, till iniquity was
found in thee.**

Revelation 12:3-4a
And there appeared another wonder in heaven; and behold a great
red dragon, having seven heads and ten horns, and seven crowns
upon his heads. **And his tail drew the third part of the stars of
heaven, and did cast them to the earth:**

And Luke 10:18
And he said unto them, **I beheld Satan as lightning fall from
heaven.**

Isaiah 14:12-14
How art thou fallen from heaven, 0 Lucifer, son of the morning!
how art thou cut down to the ground, which didst weaken the
nations! For thou hast said in thine heart, I will ascend into
heaven, I will exalt my throne above the stars of God: I will sit
also upon the mount of the congregation, in the sides of the north.
I will ascend above the heights of the clouds; I will be like the
most High.

I quoted all of the above scripture references to underscore my
point, now that I am back to the problem I have in today's Bible
with Psalm 115:16b that says, **"...but the earth hath he given to
the children of men."** The problem I have with that scripture,
is: Why would today's Bible say he gave the earth to the children

of men (us), if he had already given it to the fallen angels first? I have a problem with that. Of course God can do whatever he wants to do. He can cast down Lucifer and one-third of the fallen angels with Lucifer to earth if he wants to. But if as it says in Psalm 115:16b that God gave the earth to the children of men, how does anyone give the same thing to two different entities simultaneously? Especially when the first tenant that the earth was given to (Satan and his demon minions) has a documented history of tempting and being responsible for setting up the situation that caused the second tenant that God gave the earth to (Adam & Eve and the children of men) to fall into sin? Something just doesn't ring true with Psalm 115:16b saying God gave the earth to the children of men. When you take in THE BIG PICTURE, which includes God giving Satan run of the earth first before God was supposed to have given the earth to us humans, it seems like another contradiction to me. You can look it up in your own Bible, pray and meditate with God about it, and draw your own conclusion about it from the spirit impression that God lays on your heart. Now I will go on to point out more flaws and errors that I have found in today's Bible.

Chapter 24 - Who was Joseph's Father

<u>Compare Matthew 1:16</u>
And Jacob begat Joseph the husband of Mary, of whom was born Jesus, who is called Christ.

<u>With Luke 3:23</u>
And Jesus himself began to be about thirty years of age, being (as was supposed) the son of
Joseph, which was the son of Heli,

WELL WHICH ONE is it? Did Jacob begat Joseph, or is Joseph the son of Heli? God is not the author of confusion; therefore God would not divinely inspire having Joseph's father written down one way by one author and a different way by another author. This is another proof that makes it glaringly apparent that today's Bible has flaws and errors in it. Now I will point out another scripture reference that is somewhat confusing.

Chapter 25 - If You Seek, Will You Be Able to Find

Compare Matthew 7:7-8
Ask, and it shall be given you; **seek and ye shall find;** knock, and it shall be opened unto you: For every one that asketh receiveth; **and he that seeketh findeth;** and to him that knocketh it shall be opened.

With Luke 13:24
Strive to enter in at the strait gate: **for many, I say unto you, will seek to enter in, and shall not be able.**

IF YOU PAY attention to the part I highlighted in bold, you see that in Matthew 7:7-8, Jesus is saying seek and ye shall find, and he that seeketh findeth. But in Luke 13:24, Jesus' words say that many will seek to enter in and shall not be able. Well, which one is it? Is it, "he that seeketh findeth." Or is it, "... for many, I say unto you, will seek to enter in, and shall not be able." When you compare Jesus' words in each book of the Bible, it is inconsistent and confusing. I realize that in Luke 13:24 Jesus is telling the people in the cities and villages that in order to be saved you need to enter in at the straight gate, meaning to live a good/holy life, and in Matthew 7:7-8 Jesus was teaching on the mountain to the multitude. The problem I have with these two contradictory verses is that I don't believe God would divinely inspire it to be written down two different ways so that they appear to contradict each other because God is not the author of confusion. Now I will go on to point out another confusing and contradictory statement that is recorded in today's Bible.

Chapter 26 - Must We Love, or Hate, Our Brother

Compare 1 John 3:14-15
We know that we have passed from death unto life, because we love the brethren. **He that loveth not his brother abideth in death. Whosoever hateth his brother is a murderer:** and ye know that no murderer hath eternal life abiding in him.

With Luke 14:25-26
And there went great multitudes with him: and he turned, and said unto them; **If any man come to me, and hate not his father, and mother, and wife, and children, and brethren, and sisters, yea, and his own life also, he cannot be my disciple.**

WELL, WHICH ONE is it? If we don't love our brother we abide in death, and if we hateth our brother we are a murderer? Or when we come to Jesus we must hate our brother, sister, father, mother, and wife? The teachings measured side by side are inconsistent and confusing. God is not the author of confusion. Therefore God could not divinely inspire such confusing and seemingly contradictory statements to be recorded. Let's read on and I will point out another contradiction that I found in the Bible.

Chapter 27 - How Long Did God Design Humans to Live

Compare Genesis. 6:3
And the Lord said, My Spirit shall not always strive with man, for that he also is flesh: **yet his days shall be an hundred and twenty years.**

With Genesis 11:31-32
And Terah took Abram his son, and Lot the son of Haran his son's son, and Sarai his daughter in law, his son Abram's wife; and they went forth with them from Ur of the Chaldees, to go into the land of Canaan; and they came unto Haran, and dwelt there. **And the days of Terah were two hundred and five years: and Terah died in Haran.**

And Psalms 90:9-10
For all our days are passed away in thy wrath: we spend our years as a tale that is told. **The days of our years are threescore years and ten; and if by reason of strength they be fourscore years,** yet is their strength labour and sorrow; for it is soon cut off, and we fly away.

I'M POINTING OUT the above scripture references to show you the inconsistencies that add to the confusion in the Bible when you can see the BIG PICTURE and hold today's Bible accountable for the problems that never seem to be told to us by our clergy from the pulpit. When you compare Genesis 6:3, which quotes the Lord as saying that our days shall be one hundred and twenty years, with Genesis 11:31-32 where it says that Terah was two hundred and five years old when he died, this is confusing. If God said in Genesis 6:3 that man's days shall be one hundred and twenty years, then how did Terah live to be two hundred and five years? Was God wrong when he said man's days shall be one hundred and twenty years? Or is Terah' s age correct at two hundred and five years? There are many other men in the Old Testament who lived much longer than the one hundred and twenty years that God states shall be the number of man's days in Genesis 6:3, but I will just use Terah as an example to my point here. Then when you compare the Genesis accounts about how long a man will live, we see that Psalms 90:9-10 says the days of our years are threescore years and ten; and by reason of strength they can be fourscore years. Webster's Concise Family Dictionary says that a "score" means "twenty." Therefore, according to Psalms 90:9-10, if the days of our years are threescore and ten, that would be 70 years. The scripture adds that if by reason of strength (I believe that means if you take care of yourself through proper diet and exercise) our years of life can be fourscore, or 80 years old. These scripture references again demonstrate the confusion and inconsistency in today's Bible. They can't all be right. One (or more) of them have to be wrong. I strongly believe that God is not the author of confusion. God would not divinely inspire words to be written down one way in one account and then a different way in another account. This is more proof that today's Bible has been tampered with (interpolated).

Chapter 28 - Are Ethics Really Situational

THE FOLLOWING EXAMPLE of confusion and contradictory items in today's Bible are of a slightly different nature. They involve situational ethics. Or to put it more plainly, is it okay to commit a sin against God's laws, if the situation is a special circumstance? This type of thing has always bothered me. If it's wrong to kill, then it is wrong to kill no matter what. If it's wrong to tell a lie, then it is wrong to tell a lie no matter what. So although there aren't any direct flaws and errors in the following Bible scripture references that I am going to point out to you, the point I intend to make falls in the category of situational ethics. Another way of putting it would be: Is it sometimes okay to lie, threaten, manipulate, be sneaky, or commit treason? According to the following Bible scripture references, maybe it is okay to do these things, and violate other people's rights.

<u>1 Samuel 21:10 through 1 Samuel 22:1</u>
And David arose, and fled that day for fear of Saul, and went to Achish the king of Gath. And the servants of Achish said unto him, Is not this David the king of the land? did they not sing one to another of him in dances, saying, Saul hath slain his thousands,

and David his ten thousands? **And David laid up these words in his heart, and was sore afraid of Achish the king of Gath. And he changed his behaviour before them, and feigned himself mad in their hands, and scrabbled on the doors of the gate, and let his spittle fall down upon his beard.** Then said Achish unto his servants, Lo, ye see the man is mad: wherefore then have ye brought him to me? Have I need of mad men, that ye have brought this fellow to play the mad man in my presence? shall this fellow come into my house? David therefore departed thence, and escaped to the cave Adullam: and when his brethren and all his father's house heard it, they went down thither to him.

The above scripture reference tells the account of David in front of Achish. Apparently David lied by pretending he was a mad man. That is sneaky, and manipulative. If I were in David's shoes I might have considered doing the same thing to save myself. But here is where the situational ethics come into it. God's laws say that we should not lie. This particular Bible story doesn't have David repenting from lying. Quite the opposite. After David returned home there was a celebration. Nevertheless, I believe it was God that allowed David to be brought before Achish, and like God caused Jonah to be swallowed by a great fish and then delivered him from the belly of that great fish, God would have made a way for David to return home unharmed without David lying and playing the fool to fake his way out of there. This is one instance where the Bible seems to be teaching that it is okay to lie, depending on the reason why you are lying. That is a slippery slope that leads to destruction because each person, from their own point of view, believes they are right and justified in furthering their own cause, whatever that cause may be. The ten commandments were given to us as a standard to live up to on our spiritual path through this journey of life. If by the example of this and the following Bible stories, it tacitly implies that we can pick and choose if and when we can lie, it will lead to chaos. Let's read on to a couple other Bible stories that I will use to illustrate the point that I disagree with the situational ethics being taught in the Bible.

<u>1 Samuel 19:11-18</u>
Saul also sent messengers unto David's house, to watch him, and to slay him in the morning: and Michal David's wife told him, saying, If thou save not thy life tonight, tomorrow thou shalt be slain. So Michal let David down through a window: and he went, and fled, and escaped. **And Michal took an image, and laid it in the bed, and put a pillow of goats' hair for his bolster, and covered it with a cloth. And when Saul sent messengers to take David, she said, He is sick.** And Saul sent the messengers again to see David, saying, Bring him up to me in the bed, that I may slay him. **And when the messengers were come in, behold, there was an image in the bed, with a pillow of goats' hair for his bolster.** And Saul said unto Michal, Why hast thou deceived me so, and sent away mine enemy, that he is escaped? **And Michal answered Saul, He said unto me, Let me go: why should I kill thee?** So David fled, and escaped, and came to Samuel to Ramah, and told him all that Saul had done to him. And he and Samuel went and dwelt in Naioth.

The above scripture reference tells the account of David and the events surrounding his escape from Saul in this particular instance. You will notice in the parts that I highlighted in bold that Michal used sneaky tactics when she made up a dummy to look like David was in the bed when David had actually run away. When Saul asked Michal directly why she had deceived him so, Michal lied and said it was David's idea, when we can clearly see from the scripture that it was Michal's idea for David to save his life by fleeing. She orchestrated the whole affair and lied to Saul in an attempt to give David more time to escape. If I were in Michal's shoes; I might have considered a similar type of deception to manipulate events to turn out the way I prefered. But here again is an occasion where situational ethics were applied to go against God's law that we should not lie. This particular

Bible story doesn't have Michal repenting to God for her lying and manipulation. Here again I believe it was God that allowed David to be in the vicinity where Saul might have captured him. However, I believe that, as God caused Jonah to be swallowed by a great fish and then delivered him from the belly of the great fish, God would have made a way for David to escape from Saul without Michal being sneaky, lying, and manipulative, which is against God's law that we should not tell a lie. This is another example where the Bible seems to be teaching that it is okay to lie depending on the reason you are being sneaky and lying. It puts us in the same philosophical dilemma of the slippery slope that leads to worse and worse behavior. If humans are given tacit permission to lie whenever they feel justified, it is a slippery slope indeed. Each person, from their own point of view, believes they are right and justified in furthering their own cause, whatever that cause may be. In Exodus 20:1-18 God gives Moses the ten commandments, and I don't see anything in the chapter before it or the chapter after it, or anywhere else in the Bible, where God says it is okay to transgress his ten commandments if special circumstances arise. Eve and Adam could present a fair case of justification for why they ate fruit from the tree of knowledge of good and evil, but God wasn't having any of their justified situational ethics. God kicked them out of the garden of Eden for trying to make up their own rules.

If you look in the account of 2 Samuel 6:3-8 you will see in verse 6 that Uzzah put forth his hand to steady the ark of God because the oxen had shaken it. Uzzah thought the ark of God might fall off the ox cart and touch the ground, so Uzzah put forth his hand to steady it. In verse 7 we see that it angered God that Uzzah touched the ark, so God smote him there for his error, and Uzzah died there by the ox cart that was carrying the ark of God. Uzzah could have made a fair case of situational ethics to justify why he reached out his hand to steady the ark on the ox cart. The uneven road that the oxen were pulling the cart along shook the ark and it was in danger of toppling off. This is why Uzzah put forth his hand to steady the ark on the ox cart, but God wasn't having any situational ethics. In our human way of thinking Uzzah might have had good justification to touch the ark of God with his bare hand, but not to God's way of thinking. God struck Uzzah dead on the spot because God didn't want Uzzah to touch the ark of God with his hand.

In the following scripture reference it shows God does not take situational ethics lightly, even from one of his favored people.

<u>Numbers 20:1-13</u>
Then came the children of Israel, even the whole congregation, into the desert of Zin in the first month: and the people abode in Kadesh; and Miriam died there, and was buried there. And there was no water for the congregation: and they gathered themselves together against Moses and against Aaron. And the people chode with Moses, and spake, saying, Would God that we had died when our brethren died before the Lord! And why have ye brought up the congregation of the Lord into this wilderness, that we and our cattle should die there? And wherefore have ye made us to come up out of Egypt, to bring us in unto this evil place? It is no place of seed, or of figs, or of vines, or of pomegranates; neither is there any water to drink. And Moses and Aaron went from the presence of the assembly unto the door of the tabernacle of the congregation, and they fell upon their faces: and the glory of the Lord appeared unto them. **And the Lord spake unto Moses, saying, Take the rod, and gather thou the assembly together, thou, and Aaron thy brother, <u>and speak ye unto the rock before their eyes</u>; and it shall give forth his water, and thou shalt bring forth to them water out of the rock; so thou shalt give the congregation and their beasts drink. And Moses took the rod from before the Lord, as he commanded him.** And Moses and Aaron gathered the congregation together before the rock, and he said unto them, Hear now, ye rebels; must we fetch you water out of this rock? **And Moses lifted up his hand, <u>and</u>**

with his rod he smote the rock twice: and the water came out abundantly, and the congregation drank, and their beasts also. And the Lord spake unto Moses and Aaron, Because ye believed me not, to sanctify me in the eyes of the children of Israel, therefore ye shall not bring this congregation into the land which I have given them. This is the water of Meribah; because the children of Israel strove with the Lord, and he was sanctified in them.

The above scripture reference demonstrates that God told Moses to "speak" to the rock, but Moses "struck" the rock twice with his rod. If we were going to apply situational ethics to this incident, Moses could have easily said, "Speak to the rock or strike the rock with my rod; there's no big difference." But it did make a difference to God. When God instructed Moses to speak to the rock, that is exactly what God meant. God didn't tell Moses to strike the rock with his rod like Moses did and God was sorely displeased with Moses doing it his own way, even though Moses may have thought that the difference between speaking to the rock or striking the rock with his rod was not very big. Moses was only concerned about his people getting water. But God was concerned with obedience and following his instructions to the letter. As a consequence of Moses not following God's instructions, God told Moses, you shall not bring this congregation into the land which I have given them. Look at the following scripture reference that shows what God meant.

Deuteronomy 34:4-5
And the Lord said unto him, This is the land which I sware unto Abraham, unto Isaac, and unto Jacob, saying, I will give it unto thy seed: I have caused thee to see it with thine eyes, but thou shalt not go over thither. So Moses the servant of the Lord died there in the land of Moab, according to the word of the Lord.

This example demonstrates that God doesn't go for situational ethics. It might not seem like a big deal to us, but it is a big deal to God.

Therefore I have a problem with some of these situational ethics in the Bible that I point out to you where people in the Bible, supposedly God's people, lie when it suits them. Our human way of thinking and justifying things is not God's way, as can be seen in the following scripture.

Isaiah 55:8-9
For my thoughts are not your thoughts, neither are your ways my ways, saith the Lord. For as the heavens are higher than the earth, so are my ways higher than your ways, and my thoughts than your thoughts.

The above scripture reference clearly demonstrates that human beings are incapable of thinking on God's level. Therefore I have a problem with people of God transgressing God's laws with lying, and worse, in the Bible, and doing it with no repenting or follow up mention that it is sin to tell a lie. The following is one more instance of situational ethics in the Bible that I have a problem with.

Joshua 2:1-24
And Joshua the son of Nun sent out of Shittim two men to spy secretly, saying, Go view the land, even Jericho. And they went, and came into an harlot's house, named Rahab, and lodged there. And it was told the king of Jericho, saying, Behold, there came men in hither tonight of the children of Israel to search out the country. And the king of Jericho sent unto Rahab, saying, Bring forth the men that are come to thee, which are entered into thine house: for they be come to search out all the country. **And the woman took the two men, and hid them, and said thus, There came men unto me, but I wist not whence they were:** And it came to pass about the time of shutting of the gate, when it

was dark, that the men went out: whither the men went I wot not: **pursue after them quickly; for ye shall overtake them. But she had brought them up to the roof of the house, and hid them with the stalks of flax, which she had laid in order upon the roof.** And the men pursued after them the way to Jordan unto the fords: and as soon as they which pursued after them were gone out, they shut the gate.

And before they were laid down, she came up unto them upon the roof; And she said unto the men, I know that the Lord hath given you the land, and that your terror is fallen upon us, and that all the inhabitants of the land faint because of you. For we have heard how the Lord dried up the water of the Red sea for you, when ye came out of Egypt; and what ye did unto the two kings of the Amorites, that were on the other side Jordan, Sihon and Og, whom ye utterly destroyed. And as soon as we had heard these things, our hearts did melt, neither did there remain any more courage in any man, because of you: for the Lord your God, he is God in heaven above, and in earth beneath. **Now therefore, I pray you, swear unto me by the Lord, since I have shewed you kindness, that ye will also shew kindness unto my father's house, and give me a true token: And that ye will save alive my father, and my mother, and my brethren, and my sisters, and all that they have, and deliver our lives from death. And the men answered her, Our life for yours, if ye utter not this our business. And it shall be, when the Lord hath given us the land, that we will deal kindly and truly with thee.** Then she let them down by a cord through the window: for her house was upon the town wall, and she dwelt upon the wall. And she said unto them, Get you to the mountain, lest the pursuers meet you; and hide yourselves there three days, until the pursuers be returned: and afterward may ye go your way. And the men said unto her, We will be blameless of this thine oath which thou hast made us swear. Behold, when we come into the land, thou shalt bind this line of scarlet thread in the window which thou didst let us down by: and thou shalt bring thy father, and thy mother, and thy brethren, and all thy father's household, home unto thee. And it shall be, that whosoever shall go out of the doors of thy house into the street, his blood shall be upon his head, and we will be guiltless: and whosoever shall be with thee in the house, his blood shall be on our head, if any hand be upon him. **And if thou utter this our business, then we will be quiet of thine oath which thou has made us to swear.** And she said, According unto your words, so be it. And she sent them away, and they departed: and she bound the scarlet line in the window. And they went, and came unto the mountain, and abode there three days, until the pursuers were returned: and the pursuers sought them throughout all the way, but found them not. So the two men returned, and descended from the mountain, and passed over, and came to Joshua the son of Nun, and told him all things that befell them: And they said unto Joshua, Truly the Lord hath delivered into our hands all the land; for even all the inhabitants of the country do faint because of us.

And Joshua 6:21-27

And they utterly destroyed all that was in the city, both man and woman, young and old, and ox, and sheep, and ass, with the edge of the sword. But Joshua had said unto the two men that had spied out the country, Go into the harlot's house, and bring out thence the woman, and all that she hath, as ye sware unto her. And the young men that were spies went in, and brought out Rahab, and her father, and her mother, and her brethren, and all that she had; and they brought out all her kindred, and left them without the camp of Israel. And they burnt the city with fire, and all that was therein: only the silver, and the gold, and the vessels of brass and of iron, they put into the treasury of the house of the Lord. **And Joshua saved Rahab the harlot alive, and her father's household, and all that she had; and she dwelleth in Israel even unto this day; because she hid the messengers, which Joshua sent to spy out Jericho.**

And Joshua adjured them at that time, saying, Cursed be the man before the Lord, that riseth up and buildeth this city Jericho: he shall lay the foundation thereof in his firstborn, and in his youngest son shall he set up the gates of it. So the Lord was with Joshua; and his fame was noised throughout all the country.

As you can see from the above scripture references, there is a lot of spying, scheming, lying, and double-dealing going on. Starting at Joshua 2:1 we see Joshua sending out two spies to spy out the land of Jericho. Then in the next part of Joshua 2 that I have highlighted in bold, we see the two spies meeting a harlot and hiding in her house. Yet in 2 Corinthians 6:14 the Bible says, "Be ye not unequally yoked together with unbelievers: for what fellowship hath righteousness with unrighteousness? and what communion hath light with darkness?" How do we judge the behavior of the two spies in light of God's word in 2 Corinthians 6:14? Not only were the two spies purposely talking with a harlot, but they were also staying in her house. How do we judge that behavior that the spies are demonstrating in light of God's word in 1 Thessalonians 5:22 that says, "Abstain from all appearance of evil."

I know that in the Old Testament they were under the LAW, while in the New Testament we are in the dispensation of GRACE. Therefore some might say we shouldn't judge the Old Testament scripture references. However, this is not necessarily the case. Inappropriate behavior is inappropriate behavior in any age. God and God's law, as stated in the Old Testament Ten Commandments in Exodus 20:1-18, stands for appropriate good behavior at all times, no matter what age or dispensation we are in, up to and including this present age. God doesn't change how he wants his people to behave as faithful children of God.

Malachi 3:6a
For I am the Lord, I change not;

Hebrews 13:8
Jesus Christ the same yesterday, and to day, and for ever.

God hasn't changed. It is human beings who erroneously think it is okay to lower their standards and change their behavior with the times. I was born in the 1940s and as I was growing up I often heard people trying to influence other people to lower their standards and change by saying things like, "Get with it man, this is the 60s." "Drop out and turn on." Or, "Hey dude, this is the 70s, so we don't have to listen to the 'man'." "Hell no we won't go!" Or, "It's the 80s (or 90s) and this isn't your parents' generation any more so get in step." This tactic is put out by those who want to cause social engineering to move in a direction that benefits their own personal agenda. In order to promote their current agenda they have to disparage the old ways. But any step we take that is AWAY from God is a wrong step. It isn't God that needs to change or get in step with today's times. It is us that need to maintain our Godly character and integrity, when the rest of the world is going to hell in a handbasket. Just because the world is deep in sinful behavior and pretending it is okay, doesn't make it okay. Each and every one of us need to have a deep, personal one on one relationship with God almighty. We need to base our values and beliefs on Godly standards. We cannot let the world that is out of step with God desensitize us, as if out of step behavior is okay because we are in the new millennium. This is why I don't hesitate to judge the behavior of any age by Godly standards.

I won't comment much about Rahab's lying. After all, she is an unbeliever and also a harlot, so lying was not unusual for her anyway. She has nothing to lose by dealing with the two spies. If they come and take the city, she and her family are saved. If they come and lose the battle trying to take the city, then she doesn't have to tell her fellow citizens that she was in cahoots with the foreign invaders. Either way, she makes out okay. Being a wheeling dealing harlot already, I'm sure she knows how to scheme and try to get her bread buttered on both sides every chance she can.

So I will mostly fault the believing children of God for their transgression of God's laws. God's laws don't say anything about making an exception to transgress that law, making it okay to spy, lie, consort and conspire with harlots. If you notice the last part of Joshua 2:1-24 where I highlighted it in bold, the words of the two spies say, "And if thou utter this our business, then we will be quiet of thine oath which thou hast made us to swear." So not only are the two spies being unequally yoked with a harlot, then they turn around and threaten her that if she doesn't remain silent in the conspiracy for her to commit treason against her own people, then when the battle is going on they will come to her house and kill her and all her family. Is this how the people of God are supposed to behave? Does the end justify the means? Is this how God works? I have a real problem with this example of situational ethics that I see in the Bible. It's as if it is okay to break God's laws if you think you have a good enough reason. Now if I was Rahab, and in Rahab's shoes, I might have done similarly in order to save my own skin. I do not fault her for her behavior because she didn't believe in the God of Abraham anyway. She was a harlot and scuffling to get along for herself the best way she could. But I have serious problems accepting that it is okay for the God-believing descendants of Abraham to be spying, lying, scheming, and double-dealing in order to further their own cause. God created the universe, including earth and everything in it. Surely if God wanted Joshua and his people to have some decent land he could have given them their own land and placed them in it without promising them land that he had already given to another people first. That behavior is frightfully similar to that which I pointed out in Psalms 115:15-16, where it says, "...but the earth hath he given to the children of men."

Well yes, God gave the earth to the children of men, after he had given it to Satan and one-third of the angels that had fallen first and were thereafter occupying earth where they could exert their demonic temptations on the human race. In light of all the flaws and errors I have pointed out to you in the beginning of this book, and the various interpolations I have found to question, I have a hard time believing this double-dealing pattern is the character and nature of God Almighty. And the decisions of the Nicene Council in the year 325 A.D. on which books were going to be included "in" the Bible, and which books were going to be left "out" of the Bible, plus the subsequent changes and revisions that have been made since the Bible was originally divinely inspired and handed down to us, cause me to question today's Bible and its authenticity. How could Constantine and his cabal get together in Nicene in the year 325 A.D. and decide (for God) which books were "in" the Bible and which books were "out?" Anyway, getting back to Rahab and the two spies, I don't believe God is a double-dealer. At the same time I will say that I believe God can do whatever he wants to do. It's his ball game and he can call the shots any way he sees fit. It's just what I know of the character and nature of God in my own life experiences, I don't see God being a double-dealer, as is pointed out in Psalms 115:15-16 and in Joshua 2:1-24. I present this material to you in my book, not to tell you how it is. No. I present all this different material in my book so you can look it up for yourself and pray to God about it, inviting God's Holy Spirit to merge with your own spirit in your heart, to help guide you into the truth as to whether today's Bible has flaws and errors in it and has been interpolated or not. It is up to you to make up your own mind about today's Bible. Now I will go on to point out another scripture reference that I have a problem with.

Chapter 29 - Exactly When Did God Create Adam's Mate, Eve, for Him

Compare Genesis 2:20
And Adam gave names to all cattle, and to the fowl of the air, and to every beast of the field; **but for Adam there was not found an help meet for him.**

With Genesis 1:27
So God created man in his own image, in the image of God created he him; **male and female created he <u>them</u>.**

GOD DIVINELY INSPIRED Moses to write down Genesis, which is the chronological sequence of events that took place when God created the earth and put all things in the earth. Earlier in this book I pointed out a couple problems I have with the account of Genesis. In this instance, the problem I have is with the chronological sequence of events. Over in chapter 2, verse 20, it says there was <u>not</u> a help meet for Adam. We know this means Adam didn't have a female counterpart to keep him company. However, earlier in chapter 1, verse 27, it says God created man, male and female created he <u>them</u>. So how does that match up with later events written down in Genesis about creation, where in chapter 2, verse 20, it says Adam doesn't have a female counterpart? Genesis 1:27 clearly states that God created man, male and female he created them. So if God had created man in his own image, male and female he created_them, then why in Genesis 2:20 does it say Adam doesn't have his female counterpart yet? Something doesn't add up here. And since God is not the author of confusion, I don't believe it is God's fault. I believe that when God divinely inspired Moses to write down the creation account in Genesis, God's Holy Spirit caused it to be written down without confusing the chronological sequence of events. Today's Bible has been interpolated and I am proving it in my book. It's as simple as that.

Chapter 30 - Was Jesus Unjust

NOW I WILL point out another scripture reference that I have a problem with.

Mark 11:11-14
And Jesus entered into Jerusalem, and into the temple: and when he had looked round about upon all things, and now the eventide was come, he went out unto Bethany with the twelve. And on the morrow, when they were come from Bethany, he was hungry: **And seeing a fig tree afar off having leaves, he came, if haply he might find any thing thereon: and when he came to it, he found nothing but leaves, for the time of figs was not yet.** And Jesus answered and said unto it, No man eat fruit of thee hereafter for ever. And his disciples heard it.

And Mark 11:20-24
And in the morning, as they passed by, they saw the fig tree dried up from the roots. And Peter calling to remembrance saith unto him, Master, behold, the fig tree which thou cursedst is withered away. And Jesus answering saith unto them, Have faith in God. For verily I say unto you, That whosoever shall say unto this mountain, Be thou removed, and be thou cast into the sea; and shall not doubt in his heart, but shall believe

that those things which he saith shall come to pass; he shall have whatsoever he saith. Therefore I say unto you, What things soever ye desire, when ye pray, believe that ye receive them, and ye shall have them.

The above scripture reference is well known to devout Christians. Jesus was hungry, so he went up to a fig tree looking for a fig to eat, and finding no fruit, he curses the fig tree. Then the next morning Jesus and his twelve disciples are out walking and they pass by the same fig tree and they see that the fig tree is withered and dried up from the roots. Then Jesus responds that faith can move mountains. Well I for one strongly believe, and have, mountain moving faith. However, the part of the above scripture reference that I have a problem with is the part in Mark 11:11-14 where it says, "...he found nothing but leaves, for the time of figs was not yet..." I have never known Jesus to be unjust, and that is why I look with a skeptical eye on that particular part in today's Bible. If it was not yet time for the figs to be on the fig tree, then why would Jesus be angry about it? The fig tree was behaving exactly the way the creator God Almighty had made the fig tree to be. That is not a reason to curse the fig tree. It is beyond a fig tree, or any other fruit tree, to produce fruit prematurely. It would have been contrary to science for the fig tree to produce fruit out of season. In order for the fig tree to produce fruit before its time to bloom and produce fruit, Jesus would have had to perform a miracle. Jesus didn't have any trouble performing a miracle in Mark 6:34-44 when he took five loaves of bread and two fishes and multiplied them into enough loaves and fishes to feed five thousand men. Not only did he feed five thousand men with five loaves of bread and two fishes, but after everyone ate their fill, they took up twelve baskets full of leftovers. I personally believe that Jesus returned the twelve baskets of leftovers to the boy who offered his five loaves and two fishes to Jesus as an offering in the first place. I can just imagine the boy taking his haul home and explaining to his mother how he went out with the five loaves and two fish that she packed for him, yet he returned with twelve baskets full of fish and bread. That example just goes to show that you can't outgive God. God always multiplies the seed we sow and returns more back to us.

So if God is a just God, and God blesses us back when we make tithes and offerings into an anointed ministry, as had happened to the boy with five loaves and two fishes, then how does that generous character of God fit in with punishing a mere fig tree for behaving exactly how the creator God almighty created it to behave? I am very suspicious about that particular part in today's Bible. I believe it has been tampered with from its original text, even though I can't prove it directly. I can only speculate about how it runs contrary to the nature of God to punish a helpless fig tree that he created, for behaving exactly how he designed it to behave. Now if it were the time of figs, and that particular fig tree was the only one without any figs on it, then I could see and understand why Jesus did away with it.

Be that as it may be, I can indirectly prove that this isn't something consistent with what Jesus would do to that fig tree that didn't produce figs before its time to produce figs, by referencing Jesus' parable about a fig tree that hadn't produced any figs for three years in a row when it was the season for it to have produced figs. The following scripture reference abundantly points out and describes Jesus' attitude and behavior.

Luke 13:6-9
He spake also this parable; A certain man had a fig tree planted in his vineyard; and he came and sought fruit thereon, and found none. Then said he unto the dresser of his vineyard, Behold, these three years I come seeking fruit on this fig tree, and find none: cut it down; why cumbereth it the ground? And he answering said unto him, Lord, let it alone this year also, till I shall dig about it, and dung it: And if it bear fruit, well: And if not, then after that thou shalt cut it down.

Here we see Jesus teaching his philosophy by the example of a parable on how we should have patience and treat one another kindly and with patience, as our Father God treats us with kindness and patience. I like to personalize the Bible, and you can do the same by letting us represent the fig trees. The owner of the fig trees represents God and how God expects us to ultimately produce a fruitful life by following Godly commandments and principles. Jesus himself is represented by the dresser of the vineyard, since the dresser intercedes with the Lord of the vineyard on behalf of the fig tree that hasn't produced any fruit for three seasons in a row. Jesus intercedes and asks the Lord to give the fig tree another chance. The dresser said he will add dung and dig it in around that tree with special care in hopes that it will produce fruit the next season when it is time for figs, if the Lord will be patient and withhold judgment one more year. This example of the fig tree in Luke 13:6-9 is a powerful lesson of how God has patience with us and our less than perfect fruit-producing lives. When we compare this parable of Luke 13 about the non-producing fig tree, with his attitude and behavior in the Mark 11 description, when it wasn't even the time for figs to be on the fig tree, it flies in the face of the example Jesus himself set. Therefore I am suspicious of, and have a problem with, the Mark 11 scripture. I have to examine these two contrary scripture references (Mark 11 and Luke 13), and use the brain that God blessed me with to come to my own conclusion regarding this conundrum. When I compare these differing scripture references side by side, pray and ask God's Spirit to quicken my own spirit, to guide me to the truth of the matter, I believe that the Luke 13:6-9 account more accurately demonstrates the attitude and behavior of Jesus and all that he stands for as an intercessor (and sacrificial lamb) between God and mankind. This is more apparent if we look at it metaphorically, as if we are all God's fig trees.

However, by the way it is written in today's Bible saying, "... for the time of figs was not yet..." I have a real problem with it. I suspect that particular scripture has been tampered with from how it was written in its original divinely inspired text. If this account about the fig tree being cursed and destroyed by Jesus even though it was not yet the time for figs to be on the tree, were the only flaw or problem I had with today's Bible, I could overlook it and accept it. Jesus must have had a reason that I don't know about and the Bible doesn't explain. In that light, I could accept this one item without making too big of a deal out of it. But when you take this account of the cursing of the fig tree along with all the other flaws, errors, and interpolations that I have pointed out in my book, then I cannot just overlook it. When we look at the fig tree incident in light of all the other problems I have pointed out that I have with today's Bible, it is reasonable to consider that this fig tree account has also been tampered with from its original text. Now I will go on to point out another scripture reference that gives me pause.

Chapter 31 - Did the Gospel Writers Write Hearsay

<u>Luke 1:1-3</u>
Forasmuch as many have taken in hand to set forth in order a declaration of those things which are most surely believed among us. **Even as they delivered them unto us, which from the beginning were eyewitnesses, and ministers of the word;** It seemed good to me also, having had perfect understanding of all things from the very first, to write unto thee in order, most excellent Theophilus.

MY FIRST THOUGHT about the scripture reference in Luke 1:1-3 is, what exactly is he trying to say? I believe Luke is saying there are no Gospels written by the Apostles themselves. Where Luke says, "... Even as they delivered them unto us, which from the beginning were eyewitnesses, and ministers of the word..." I believe Luke is making a distinction between the Gospel writers and the eyewitnesses, the Apostles. It sounds like he is saying that he in person examined the facts from the original source. Is that Luke's way of making his account sound more authentic? When I slow down and examine the above scripture reference, it takes a lot of thinking to unscramble exactly what Luke is trying to say. At least for me it takes a lot of thinking to try and sort it out. When I just read it over once lightly, it is so "busy" in its verbiage that its true meaning doesn't really sink in. When you slow down and examine the above scripture reference from Luke, see if you also think he is saying what I think he is saying, that he personally examined the facts from the original source. If that is indeed what he is saying, then he is admitting that he didn't witness any of it firsthand.

So if Luke didn't see firsthand the accounts he wrote in the book of Luke, then really how accurate are his accounts? It's almost as if when they were written, the authors didn't know that the four Gospels would be joined together as part of a larger book, where each account could be examined side by side. Jesus didn't leave his own written record behind, nor did he instruct any of his disciples to write down a written record. So when we look at the overall BIG PICTURE, it is easier to understand why these flaws and inconsistencies are in the Gospels of today's Bible. Now I will point out another scripture reference that gives more validation that the Gospel writers didn't witness what they were writing about firsthand.

John 19:33-36
But when they came to Jesus, and saw that he was dead already, they brake not his legs: But one of the soldiers with a spear pierced his side, and forthwith came there out blood and water. **And he that saw it bare record, and his record is true: and he knoweth that he saith true,** that ye might believe. For these things were done, that the scripture should be fulfilled, A bone of him shall not be broken.

The above scripture reference from John 19:33-36 is a little bit easier to understand, than it was for me to sort out what Luke was saying in Luke 1:1-3. If you pay special attention to the part that I put in bold highlight, it speaks quite plainly that whoever did see it firsthand (the account John is writing about) is the one who bares the record and claims it is true. Then the Gospel writer John comes along and writes this Gospel account about something he himself didn't see firsthand. So how accurate can this stuff be? Don't forget the example I used earlier in my book about President John F. Kennedy being assassinated only 50 years ago, and look at all the conflicting stories there are out there about that event. Those conflicting stories start with the eye witnesses, then are told and retold. Even if the eye witnesses were accurate in telling what they saw firsthand, the stories expand or contract with each subsequent retelling. Now we look at the Gospels which are approximately 2000 years old, and we see the Gospel writers themselves saying they are writing about accounts that they are hearing from someone else who "claims" to be an eye witness. When you pray and meditate with God about these things, ask the Holy Spirit to enlighten your understanding and lead you into the truth, so you can make up your own mind, as to whether you agree, or not, that today's Bible has flaws, errors, and interpolations in it. Keep in mind when you pray for insight over the above scripture reference of John 19:33-36, that if John saw firsthand what he is writing about in his Gospel, he would not have said, "…he that saw it bare record, and his record is true…" And ask yourself, is your clergy pointing these things out to you from the pulpit of your home church? Now I will go on to point out another inconsistency that I find in today's Bible.

Chapter 32 - Did John Come Neither Eating or Drinking

<u>Compare Matthew 3:1-4</u>
In those days came John the Baptist, preaching in the wilderness of Judaea, And saying, Repent ye: for the kingdom of heaven is at hand. For this is he that was spoken of by the prophet Esaias, saying, The voice of one crying in the wilderness, Prepare ye the way of the Lord, make his paths straight. And the same John had his raiment of camel's hair, and a leathern girdle about his loins; **and his meat was locusts and wild honey.**

<u>With Matthew 11:12-18</u>
And from the days of John the Baptist until now the kingdom of heaven suffereth violence, and the violent take it by force. For all the prophets and the law prophesied until John. And if ye will receive it, this is Elias, which was for to come. He that hath ears to hear, let him hear. But whereunto shall I liken this generation? It is like unto children sitting in the markets, and calling unto their fellows, And saying, We have piped unto you, and ye have not danced; we have mourned unto you, and ye have not lamented. **For John came neither eating nor drinking,** and they say, He hath a devil.

WHEN YOU COMPARE Matthew 3:1-4 with Matthew 11:12-18, paying special attention to the part that I highlighted in bold, you will see a contradiction. In Matthew's account in 3:1-4, he said John the Baptist's meat, or food, was locusts and wild honey. But in Matthew 11:12-18, where it is Jesus speaking, Jesus says that John came neither eating nor drinking. So which one is right? Can they both be right when they contradict each other? And if one of them is right, then the other one, by process of elimination, has to be wrong. The above scripture reference is another flaw that I see in today's Bible. God is not the author of confusion. When God's Holy Spirit divinely inspires a person to write something down, he doesn't forget that on one account he divinely inspired it to be written one way, and then divinely inspires another person to write it in a different way. Either John the Baptist ate locusts and wild honey for his food, or John came neither eating nor drinking. This is another flaw that I find in today's Bible, and I don't believe it is God's fault. I believe the original Bible that the Holy Spirit divinely inspired to be written by the original authors of the Bible, has been tampered with and interpolated. The above two scripture references that describe the same John the Baptist contradict each other. This is one more proof that you can look up in your own Bible, and, praying and meditating with God for guidance and direction, make up your own mind if today's Bible is interpolated or not. Let's read on to contemplate more contradictions that are in today's Bible.

Chapter 33 - Do We Teach/Baptize, or Give Not, God's Commands to the Unsaved

Compare Matthew 7:6
Give not that which is holy unto the dogs, neither cast ye your pearls before swine, lest they trample them under their feet, and turn again and rend you.

With Matthew 28:18-20
And Jesus came and spake unto them, saying, All power is given unto me in heaven and earth. **Go ye therefore, and teach all nations, baptizing them in the name of the Father, and of the Son, and of the Holy Ghost: Teaching them to observe all things whatsoever I have commanded you:** and, lo, I am with you alway, even unto the end of the world. Amen.

IN THE FIRST Matthew 7:6 scripture reference, we see Jesus speaking to his disciples. Jesus is telling his disciples not to teach the "dogs," which was the term used to describe unbelievers or people of faith other than the faith of Jesus and his followers. The faith of Jesus was Jewish. Where the confusing part comes in is when you compare the part in Matthew 7:6 that I highlighted in bold, with the part in Matthew 28:18-20 that I highlighted in bold where Jesus is saying, Go and teach all nations all things whatsoever I have commanded you. Well which is it? Don't give it to the dogs? Those outside of the faith? Or go and give it to all of them? I know that Jesus made a way to bring all the gentiles to come and believe in God Almighty. Gentile is a term also used for pagan non-believers. But if God is not the author of confusion, then why would God have the Holy Spirit divinely inspire the author of Matthew to write down in one part that the disciples should not give holy things to dogs, neither cast your pearls before swine, and then in another part of Matthew inspire it to be written down that the disciples were supposed to teach all pagans from every nation, so that they might get converts to baptize in the name of the Father, Son, and Holy Ghost? Whatever the reason for the confusing statements, I don't believe it is God's fault. The problem with the contradictions and flaws in today's Bible is due to human tampering (writing that wasn't divinely inspired by God). Let's read on about other scripture references that I have a problem with.

Compare Matthew 10:5-6
These twelve Jesus sent forth, and commanded them, saying, **Go not into the way of the Gentiles, and into any city of the Samaritans enter ye not: But go rather to the lost sheep of the house of Israel.**

With Matthew 24:13-14
But he that shall endure unto the end, the same shall be saved. **And this gospel of the kingdom shall be preached in all the world for a witness unto all nations;** and then the end come.

In the above two scripture references we have the same dilemma as we had with the two scripture references prior to these two. If you pay special attention to the part in Matthew 10:5-6 that I highlighted in bold, we have Jesus recorded as saying not to go to the Gentiles or Samaritans. But then in Matthew 24:13-

14, when you observe the part that I highlighted in bold, we have Jesus recorded as saying this gospel of the kingdom shall be preached in all the world. Well which is it? Surely all the rest of the world is made up of Gentiles and Samaritans. Since God is not the author of confusion, God would not instruct the Holy Spirit to cause the author of this book of the Bible to record one thing in one part of the book, and then divinely inspire it to be recorded differently in another part of this book of the Bible. God is infallible. I will not believe it is God's fault that these two confusing and contradictory statements are in the Bible. I believe that today's Bible has been tampered with by men who weren't inspired by God, and is interpolated. Now let's read on as I show you another problem I have with today's Bible.

Chapter 34 - Who Really Begat, or Was the Son, of Who

<u>Compare Luke 3:27</u>
Which was the son of Joanna, which was the son of Rhesa, which was the son of Zorobabel, which was the son of **Salathiel, which was the Son of Neri.**

<u>With Matthew 1:12</u>
And after they were brought to Babylon, **Jechonias begat Salathiel;** and Salathiel begat Zorobabel.

THESE GENEALOGIES CAN be overwhelming if you really try to follow them closely. When we look at Luke 3:27 we see that Neri begat Salathiel. But when we look at Matthew 1:12 we see that Jechonias begat Salathiel. Yet both Luke 3:27 and Matthew 1:12 agree that Salathiel begat Zorobabel. So when it comes to who begat Salathiel, which one was it? Was it Neri? Or was it Jechonias? When you compare the part that I highlighted in bold in Luke 3:27 and in Matthew 1:12, it is glaringly apparent that there is an error. This is just one more proof that today's Bible has mistakes in it. I will also again reassert that any mistakes in today's Bible are not God's fault. It is the fault of the uninspired human beings who tampered with God's divinely inspired Word that he gave to the original authors of the Bible. Let's read on and I will show you more proof that today's Bible has been tampered with. Let's read on to contemplate more problems I have with today's Bible.

<u>Compare Luke 3: 35-36</u>
Which was the son of Saruch, which was the son of Ragau, which was the son of Phalec, which was the son of Heber, which was the son of **Sala, Which was the son of Cainan, which was the son of Arphaxad,** which was the son of Sem, which was the son of Noe, which was the son of Lamech,

<u>With 1 Chronicles 1:17-18</u>
The sons of Shem; Elam, and Asshur, **and Arphaxad,** and Lud and Aram, and Uz, and Hul, and Gether, and Meshech. **And Arphaxad begat Shelah,** and Shelah begat Eber.

<u>And Also With Genesis 11:10-15</u>
These are the generations of Shem: **Shem was an hundred years old, and begat Arphaxad** two years after the flood: And Shem lived after he begat Arphaxad five hundred years, and begat sons and daughters. **And Arphaxad lived five and thirty years, and begat Salah:** And Arphaxad lived after he begat Salah four hundred and three years, and begat sons and daughters. **And Salah lived thirty years, and begat Eber:** And Salah lived after he begat Eber four hundred and three years, and begat sons and daughters.

Let's look at the parts in the above scripture references that I highlighted in bold. When you compare Luke 3:35-36 with 1 Chronicles 1:17-18 and also Genesis 11:10-15, we see that Sala (also spelled Salah or Shelah) in Luke was the grandson of Arphaxad. But when you examine the genealogies in 1 Chronicles 1:17-18 and Genesis 11:10-15, we see that Sala/Salah/Shelah was the son of Arphaxad. In the 1 Chronicles 1:17-18 and Genesis 11:10-15, there is no mention of Cainan being the son of Arphaxad. Yet all three accounts say that Heber (also Eber) was the son of Sala. So what is the correct information? Is Sala the son or grandson of Arphaxad? It cannot be both ways. Whichever one is right, then the other one, by process of elimination, has to be wrong.

Since God is not the author of confusion, I don't believe God would divinely inspire the genealogies of anyone to be written one way in one part of the Bible, then divinely inspire it to be written a different way in another part of the Bible. This is one more proof that I have to demonstrate that today's Bible has been tampered with, from the original Bible that God caused to be written down. Now I will show you another scripture reference that I have a problem with.

Chapter 35 - Who Did or Didn't Ascend Up to Heaven

<u>Compare John 3:13</u>
And no man hath ascended up to heaven, but he that came down from heaven, even the Son of man which is in heaven.

<u>With Genesis 5:21-24</u>
And Enoch lived sixty and five years, and begat Methuselah: And Enoch walked with God after he begat Methuselah three hundred years, and begat sons and daughters: And all the days of Enoch were three hundred sixty and five years: **And Enoch walked with God: and he was not; for God took him.**

<u>And With 2 Kings 2:9-13</u>
And it came to pass, when they were gone over, that Elijah said unto Elisha, Ask what I shall do for thee, before I be taken away from thee. And Elisha said, I pray thee, let a double portion of thy spirit be upon me. And he said, Thou hast asked a hard thing: nevertheless, if thou see me when I am taken from thee, it shall be so unto thee; but if not, it shall not be so. And it came to pass, as they still went on, and talked, that, **behold, there appeared a chariot of fire, and horses of fire, and parted them both asunder; and Elijah went up by a whirlwind into heaven.** And

Elisha saw it, and he cried, My father, my father, the chariot of Israel, and the horsemen thereof. And he saw him no more: and he took hold of his own clothes, and rent them in two pieces. He took up also the mantle of Elijah that fell from him, and went back, and stood by the bank of Jordan:

IN THE FIRST scripture reference of John 3:13 we see Jesus speaking to Nicodemus, saying, "...No man hath ascended up to heaven, but he that came down from heaven..." But in Genesis 5:21-24 we see that Enoch was miraculously taken up to heaven, because one moment Enoch was walking with God, and the next moment he was not, for God took him. Then in 2 Kings 2:9-13, if you focus primarily on the part that I highlighted in bold, you see that Elijah was taken up to heaven in a whirlwind. How can that be if Jesus is saying in John 3:13 that no man ascends up to heaven but he that came down from heaven? It is confusing, and God is not the author of confusion. Therefore something doesn't add up and I don't believe it is God's fault. God wouldn't divinely inspire confusion and contradictory statements to be written down in his Holy Bible like we find in today's Bible. Today's Bible has been rewritten and interpolated. That is why there are so many flaws and errors in it. All the decades that I've attended different Christian churches of many different denominations, trying to find myself a home church, I would hear the clergy in the pulpit say the Bible was written in a simple way so that anyone can understand it. But after the service, or at a Wednesday afternoon Bible study group, when I would bring some of the problems I have with the Bible up to the clergy, he would say that I don't understand. Well if the Bible was written in a simple form so the common average person can understand it, then why do so many laity in the membership not understand today's Bible? I believe today's Bible is hard to understand because the original divinely inspired Holy Bible has been rewritten and interpolated.

Now I will point out some more scripture references that I have a problem with.

Chapter 36 - Why Would Luke Omit the Historically Meaningful

<u>Compare Matthew 1:6</u>
And Jesse begat David the king; and **David the king begat Solomon** of her that had been the wife of Urias.

<u>With Luke 3:31-32a</u>
Which was the son of Melea, which was the son of Menan, which was the son of Mattatha, which was the son of **Nathan, which was the son of David,** which was the son of Jesse.

IF YOU LOOK at the part of each scripture that I highlighted in bold, you will see in Matthew 1:6 that king David begat Solomon. This is a well known account. Not only is it well documented in 2 Samuel 11:1-27, about how king David saw and took Bathsheba away from Uriah the Hittite, but it is also well documented in 1 Kings 2:12, about how Solomon sat upon the throne after his father, David, died. Even Hollywood has made numerous movies about king David and Solomon. But when we look at Luke's genealogy account, we see that Luke lists Nathan as the son of David, not bothering to make any mention of David's greatest son, king Solomon. It leads me to wonder and be suspicious as to how knowledgeable and accurate the Gospels really are that we have in today's Bible. We cannot back away from the fact that God is not the author of confusion (1 Corinthians 14:33). God would not confuse us by divinely inspiring one thing to be written down in one book of the Bible and then cause it to be written down a different way in another book of the Bible, because that is confusing. Let's read on as I point out more scripture references from today's Bible that I have a problem with.

Chapter 37 - Why Was Imannuel Named Jesus

Compare Isaiah 7:14
Therefore the Lord himself shall give you a sign; Behold, a virgin shall conceive, and bear a son, **and shall call his name Immanuel.**

With Matthew 1:18-25
Now the birth of Jesus Christ was on this wise: When as his mother Mary was espoused to Joseph, before they came together, she was found with child of the Holy Ghost. When Joseph, her husband, being a just man, and not willing to make her a publick example, was minded to put her away privily. But while he thought on these things, behold, the angel of the Lord appeared unto him in a dream, saying, Joseph, thou son of David, fear not to take unto thee Mary thy wife; for that which is conceived in her is of the Holy Ghost. And she shall bring forth a son, and **thou shalt call his name JESUS:** for he shall save his people from their sins. Now all this was done, that it might be fulfilled which was spoken of the Lord by the prophet, saying, Behold, a virgin shall be with child, and shall bring forth a son, **and they shall call his name Emmanuel,** which being interpreted is, God with us.

Then Joseph being raised from sleep did as the angel of the Lord had bidden him, and took unto him his wife: And knew her not till she had brought forth her firstborn son: **and he called his name JESUS.**

<u>With Luke 1:26-31</u>
And in the sixth month the angel Gabriel was sent from God unto a city of Galilee, named Nazareth, To a virgin espoused to a man whose name was Joseph, of the house of David; and the virgin's name was Mary. And the angel came in unto her, and said, Hail, thou that art highly favoured, the Lord is with thee: blessed art thou among women. And when she saw him, she was troubled at his saying, and cast in her mind what manner of salutation this should be. And the angel said unto her, Fear not, Mary: for thou hast found favour with God. And behold, thou shalt conceive in thy womb, and bring forth a son, **and shalt call his name JESUS.**

WHEN WE LOOK at Isaiah 7:14 we see the prophecy of a virgin conceiving a son, and shall call his name Immanuel. Common sense says that in order for the prophecy in Isaiah 7:14 to be fulfilled, a virgin would conceive a son and call his name Immanuel. However, when we look at Matthew 1:18-25, we see Joseph having a dream where an angel appears to him and tells him to take Mary for his wife, for she is conceived by the Holy Ghost and will have a son who shall be called JESUS. Matthew adds that all this was done so that the prophecy of Isaiah 7:14 can be fulfilled, where a virgin has a son, and the son shall be named Emmanuel. Then we go to Luke 1:26-31, and see that Mary was visited by the angel Gabriel, and Gabriel told Mary that she will conceive a son and shall call his name Jesus. The problem I have with all of this is that the Isaiah 7:14 prophecy says the son's name shall be Immanuel. Matthew even points out in Matthew 1:18-25 that all this is being done in order to fulfill the prophecy of a virgin bearing a son, and they shall call his name Emmanuel. Therefore we have both in the Old Testament of Isaiah 7:14 specifically stating that the child's name shall be Immanuel, and in the New Testament in Matthew 1:18-25 that the prophecy says they shall call his name Emmanual. So there is no problem in the translation from Old Testament to the New Testament, as both the Old and New Testaments clearly state that they shall call his name Immanuel/Emmanuel. But they called his name JESUS, not Immanuel/Emmanuel. This is confusing. God is not the author of confusion. God would not cause the Holy Spirit to divinely inspire Isaiah to prophecy that his name shall be Immanuel, and then change it to Jesus in the New Testament, since God is not the author of confusion. So this is one more thing that I point out that I have a problem with in today's Bible. Now I will point out more scripture references that I have a problem with.

Chapter 38 - Was John the Baptist, Elias

<u>Compare Luke 1:11-17</u>
And there appeared unto him an angel of the Lord standing on the right side of the altar of incense. And when Zacharias saw him, he was troubled, and fear fell upon him. But the angel said unto him, Fear not, Zacharias: for thy prayer is heard; and thy wife Elisabeth shall bear thee a son, and thou shalt call his name John. And thou shalt have joy and gladness; and many shall rejoice at his birth. For he shall be great in the sight of the Lord, and shall drink neither wine nor strong drink; and he shall be filled with the Holy Ghost, even from his mother's womb. And many of the children of Israel shall he turn to the Lord their God. **And he shall go before him in the spirit and power of Elias,** to turn the hearts of the fathers to the children, and the disobedient to the wisdom of the just; to make ready a people prepared for the Lord.

<u>With Matthew 11:7-14</u>
And as they departed, Jesus began to say unto the multitudes concerning John, What went ye out into the wilderness to see? A reed shaken with the wind? But what went ye out for to see? A

146

man clothed in soft raiment? behold, they that wear soft clothing are in kings' houses. But what went ye out for to see? A prophet? yea, I say unto you, and more than a prophet. **For this is he,** of whom it is written, Behold, I send my messenger before thy face, which shall prepare thy way before thee. Verily I say unto you, Among them that are born of woman there hath not risen a greater than John the Baptist: notwithstanding he that is least in the kingdom of heaven is greater than he. And from the days of John the Baptist until now the kingdom of heaven suffereth violence, and the violent take it by force. For all the prophets and the law prophesied until John. And if ye will receive it, **this is Elias, which was for to come.**

<u>And Matthew 17:10-13</u>
And his disciples asked him, saying, Why then say the scribes that Elias must first come? And Jesus answered and said unto them, Elias truly shall first come, and restore all things. **But I say unto you, That Elias is come already,** and they knew him not, but have done unto him whatsoever they listed. Likewise shall also the Son of man suffer of them. <u>Then the disciples understood that he spake unto them of John the Baptist.</u>

<u>And John 1:19-28</u>
And this is the record of John, when the Jews sent priests and Levites from Jerusalem to ask him, Who art thou? And he confessed, and denied not; but confessed, I am not the Christ. **And they asked him, What then? Art thou Elias? And he saith, I am not. Art thou that prophet? And he answered, No.** Then said they unto him, Who art thou? that we may give an answer to them that sent us. What sayest thou of thyself? He said, I am the voice of one crying in the wilderness, Make straight the way of the lord, as said the prophet Esaias. And they which were sent were of the Pharisees. And they asked him, and said unto him, Why baptizest thou then, if thou be not that Christ, nor Elias, neither that prophet? John answered them, saying, I baptize with water: but there standeth one among you, whom ye know not; He it is,

who coming after me is preferred before me, whose shoe's latchet I am not worthy to unloose. These things were done in Bethabara beyond Jordan, where John was baptizing.

IF YOU PAY special attention to the parts in the above four scripture references that I highlighted in bold, you will see that in Luke 1:11-17, the angel told Zacharias that his wife Elizabeth shall bear a son, and this son shall go "...in the spirit and power of Elias..." I don't know about you, but if an angel appeared in the flesh to me, I would talk about it with my immediate family members and tell them exactly what the angel said. The angel said my son would go in the spirit and power of Elias, and that is what I would be telling my pregnant wife. After my wife gave birth I would be telling my child about the visitation I had from the angel and tell him everything the angel said. If I were Zacharias, I would see to it that my son, John, would know that he would go in the spirit and power of Elias. The angel didn't say John would be Elias arisen or that he would be reborn again as John, or anything like that. John is not the reincarnation of Elias. And it looks like Zacharias did a pretty good job of teaching his son John about what the angel forecast, because when we look at John 1:19-28 the priests and Levites asked John directly if he was Elias, and John said he was not. But when we look at Jesus talking about John in Matthew 11:7-14 and Matthew 17:10-13, Jesus said "For this is he..." and that "Elias is come already..." In Matthew 17:12, it is purported that Jesus said Elias is come already. In Matthew 17:13, Matthew directly points out that, "Then the disciples understood that he spake unto them of John the Baptist." Taken literally the way Matthew quoted Jesus, assuming Matthew quoted Jesus accurately, this is clearly an error. John was not Elias. Luke 1:11-17 says John went in the spirit of Elias. This might sound like splitting hairs, and to some extent it is. However, Jesus is a stickler for accuracy. Note in Matthew 11:7-14, that after Jesus says that there has not risen one greater than John the Baptist, he immediately adds for scriptural correctness, "not withstanding he that is least in the kingdom of heaven is greater than he." In that instance Jesus was staying scripturally accurate as we can see in the following scriptures.

Matthew 19:28-30
And Jesus said unto them, Verily I say unto you, That ye which have followed me, in the regeneration when the Son of man shall sit in the throne of his glory, ye also shall sit upon twelve thrones, judging the twelve tribes of Israel. And every one that hath forsaken houses, or brethren, or sisters, or father, or mother, or wife, or children, or lands, for my name's sake, shall receive an hundredfold, and shall inherit everlasting life. **But many that are first shall be last; and the last shall be first.**

So if Jesus thought it was important enough to modify what he had just said about how there has not risen one greater than John the Baptist, with the qualifier, "not withstanding he that is least in the kingdom of heaven is greater than he" then I can think it is important enough to put the flaws and errors that I have discovered in today's Bible under scrutiny. When we examine the flaws and errors that are in the Bible, let's remember that according to Jesus' words in Matthew 11:7-14, he too is a stickler for scriptural correctness. Let's read on and I will point out more scripture references in today's Bible that I have a problem with.

Chapter 39 - Was it an Ass <u>and</u> a Colt

<u>Compare Matthew 21:1-7</u>
And when they drew nigh unto Jerusalem, and were come
to Bethphage, unto the mount of Olives, then sent Jesus two
disciples, Saying unto them, Go into the village over against
you, **and straightway ye shall find an ass tied, and a colt with
her: loose <u>them</u>, and bring <u>them</u> unto me.** And if any man say
ought unto you, ye shall say, The Lord hath need of <u>them</u>; and
straightway he will send <u>them</u>. All this was done, that it might
be fulfilled which was spoken by the prophet, saying, Tell ye the
daughter of Sion, Behold, thy King cometh unto thee, meek, and
sitting upon an ass, and a colt the foal of an ass. And the disciples
went, and did as Jesus commanded them. **And brought the ass,
and the colt,** and put on them their clothes, and they set him
thereon.

<u>With Mark 11:1-7</u>
And when they came nigh to Jerusalem, unto Bethphage and
Bethany, at the mount of Olives, he sendeth forth two of his
disciples, And said unto them, Go your way into the village over
against you: and as soon as ye be entered into it, ye shall find a
colt tied, whereon never a man sat; loose <u>him</u>, and bring <u>him</u>. And
if any man say unto you, Why do ye this? say ye that the Lord

hath need of <u>him</u>; and straightway he will send <u>him</u> hither. And they went their way, and found the colt tied by the door without in a place where two ways met; and they loose <u>him</u>. And certain of them that stood there said unto them, What do ye, loosing the colt? And they said unto them even as Jesus had commanded: and they let them go. And they brought the colt to Jesus, and cast their garments on him; and he sat upon him.

<u>And Luke 19:29-35</u>
And it came to pass, when he was come nigh to Bethphage and Bethany, at the mount called the mount of Olives, he sent two of his disciples, Saying, Go ye into the village over against you; **in the which at your entering ye shall find a colt tied, whereon yet never man sat: loose <u>him</u>, and bring <u>him</u> hither.** And if any man ask you, Why do ye loose <u>him</u>? thus shall ye say unto him, Because the Lord hath need of <u>him</u>. And they that were sent went their way, and found even as he had said unto them. And as they were loosing <u>the</u> colt, the owners thereof said unto them, Why loose ye <u>the</u> colt? And they said, The Lord hath need of <u>him</u>. And they brought him to Jesus: and they cast their garments upon the colt, and they set Jesus thereon.

<u>And Also John 12:12-15</u>
On the next day much people that were come to the feast, when they heard that Jesus was coming to Jerusalem, Took branches of palm trees, and went forth to meet him, and cried, Hosanna: Blessed is the King of Israel that cometh in the name of the Lord. **And Jesus, When he had found a young ass, sat thereon; as it is written,** Fear not, daughter of Sion; behold, thy King cometh, sitting on an ass's colt.

IN MATTHEW 21:1-7, we see that Jesus told two disciples to go into the next village and find an ass tied with her colt. He told them to untie them and bring them to him. And they brought the colt and ass. But in Mark 11:1-7, Luke 19:2935, and John 12:12-15, their accounts say that Jesus told his two disciples to only find a colt, loose him, and bring him. So which version is the right version? Is the Matthew 21:1-7 version right? Or are the Mark, Luke, and John versions right? Whichever way is right, then the other way, by process of elimination, has to be wrong. This is another flaw and error that I have a problem with in today's Bible.

Chapter 40 - Did Judas Purchase Potter's Field

<u>Compare Matthew 27:1-8</u>
When the morning was come, all the chief priests and elders of the people took counsel against Jesus to put him to death: And when they had bound him, they led him away, and delivered him to Pontius Pilate the governor. Then Judas, which had betrayed him, when he saw that he was condemned, repented himself, and brought again the thirty pieces of silver to the chief priests and elders, Saying, I have sinned in that I have betrayed the innocent blood. And they said, What is that to us? see thou to that. And he cast down the pieces of silver in the temple, and departed, **and went and hanged himself. And the chief priests took the silver pieces,** and said, It is not lawful for to put them into the treasury, because it is the price of blood. And they took counsel, **and bought with them the potter's field,** to bury strangers in. Wherefore that field was called, The field of blood, unto this day.

<u>With Acts 1:16-19</u>
Men and brethren, this scripture must needs have been fulfilled, which the Holy Ghost by the mouth of David spake before

Reverend Terrance J. Shaw, Ph.D., D.D., D.B.S.

concerning Judas, which was guide to them that took Jesus. For he was numbered with us, and had obtained part of this ministry. **Now this man purchased a field with the reward of iniquity; and falling headlong, he burst asunder in the midst, and all his bowels gushed out.** And it was known unto all the dwellers at Jerusalem; insomuch as that field is called in their proper tongue, Aceldama, that is to say, The field of blood.

THE ABOVE TWO scripture references tell how Judas betrayed Jesus for thirty pieces of silver, which money was used to purchase a potter's field. But in Matthew 27:1-8, it says that Judas repented, threw down the thirty pieces of silver, hanged himself, and the chief priests bought the potter's field with the blood money. But in the Acts 1:16-19 account, it says that Judas purchased the potter's field, and then he fell headlong, (presumably off a cliff onto the rocks below) and his middle section burst open so that all of his bowels gushed out. These are two different accounts of the same incident. Did Judas hang himself? Or did Judas fall headlong, and burst his stomach open so that his guts gushed out? Did Judas buy the potter's field with the blood money after he repented? Or did the high priests purchase the potter's field? There are too many contradictions when we compare these two accounts. This brings me back to the statement that God is not the author of confusion. God wouldn't divinely inspire it to be written down one way in one part of the Bible, then divinely inspire it to be written down with different details in another part of the Bible, thereby contradicting the main points in his first account. This is one more proof that today's Bible has been tampered with from when God divinely inspired the original authors of the Bible. Now I will point out another confusing scripture reference that I have a problem with in today's Bible.

154

Chapter 41 - If You Saw a Real Miracle in Person, Would You Later Doubt

<u>Compare Matthew 3:13-17</u>
Then cometh Jesus from Galilee to Jordan unto John, to be baptized of him. **But John forbad him, saying, I have need to be baptized of thee, and comest thou to me?** And Jesus answering said unto him, Suffer it to be so now: for thus it becometh us to fulfill all righteousness. Then he suffered him. And Jesus, when he was baptized, went up straightway out of the water: **and, lo, the heavens were opened unto him, and he saw the Spirit of God descending like a dove, and lighting upon him: And lo a voice from heaven, saying, This is my beloved Son, in whom I am well pleased.**

<u>With Matthew 11:2-3</u>
Now when John had heard in the prison the works of Christ, he sent two of his disciples, **And said unto them, Art thou he that should come, or do we look for another?**

THE ABOVE TWO scripture references contradict each other in that when John baptized Jesus, John heard and saw that the heavens opened and the Spirit of God (in the form of a dove) descended upon Jesus, and a voice out of the heavens said, "... This is my beloved Son..." How many times do you think that happened to John in his baptizing career? Out of the hundreds and thousands of people that John the Baptist had baptized, how often do you think that miracle from heaven happened? Not once ever before, until he baptized Jesus, the Son of God. I know if something as dramatic as that ever happened to me, where I witnessed a real life miracle where God suspended the natural laws of nature, I'd certainly believe it and remember it and not doubt. The way it actually is for me, I have to go on faith, without me ever having actually seen the natural laws of nature suspended so that a miracle takes place right before my eyes, like it did for John the Baptist. But then in Matthew 11:2-3, after John the Baptist is in prison, he sends two of his disciples to ask Jesus if he really is the one that should come. How could it be that John had to ask that question if John himself saw the dove descend upon Jesus after John baptized him, and heard God's voice come down from heaven saying, "... This is my beloved Son..."? And that happened to John way back before electricity was discovered, so he couldn't have thought it was anything other than a miracle. If I were John the Baptist there would not be any question in my mind that Jesus was the one God sent. This is why I have a problem with these two scripture references. But the clincher is the following scripture reference, when you take it in relation to the above two scripture references.

John 1:29-34
The next day John seeth Jesus coming unto him, and saith, Behold the Lamb of God, which taketh away the sin of the world. This is he of whom I said, After me cometh a man which is preferred before me: for he was before me. And I knew him not: but that he should be made manifest to Israel, therefore am I come baptizing with water. And John bare record, saying, I saw the Spirit descending from heaven like a dove, and it abode upon

him. And I knew him not: but he that sent me to baptize with water, the same said unto me, Upon whom thou shalt see the Spirit descending, and remaining on him, the same is he which baptizeth with the Holy Ghost. **And I saw, and bare record that this is the Son of God.**

Now when we take John 1:29-34 into consideration, there can be no question that John the Baptist knew who Jesus was, and here it is recorded in John's own words that he saw, and bare record that Jesus was the Son of God. This account brings into question all the more the Matthew 11:2-3 account where John is supposed to have sent two of his disciples to question Jesus as to if he was the one they were looking for. It might have happened just the way the scripture references say, but I question John's lack of faith. Let's read on and I will point out more scripture references in today's Bible that I have a problem with.

Chapter 42 - Did Jesus Lie

AFTER I READ and meditate the following scripture references, I have to ask myself if Jesus told a lie to the brethren. Of course I believe on faith that Jesus was perfectly righteous and did not sin. That is why when I read and contemplate the following scripture reference, it gives me pause.

John 7:1-10
After these things Jesus walked in Galilee: for he would not walk in Jewry, because the Jews sought to kill him. Now the Jews' feast of tabernacles was at hand. His brethren therefore said unto him, Depart hence, and go into Judaea, that thy disciples also may see the works that thou doest. For there is no man that doeth any thing in secret, and he himself seeketh to be known openly. If thou do these things, shew thyself to the world. For neither did his brethren believe in him. **Then Jesus said unto them,** My time is not yet come: but your time is always ready. The world cannot hate you; but me it hateth, because I testify of it, that the works thereof are evil. **Go ye up unto this feast: I go not up yet unto this feast; for my time is not yet full come.** When he had said these words unto them, he abode still in Galilee. **But when his brethren were gone up, then went he also up unto the feast, not openly, but as it were in secret.**

If you pay special attention to the parts that I highlighted in bold, you will see that Jesus told the brethren that he wasn't going to go up to the feast, but after his brethren leave, then he goes up to the feast incognito. I guess if he went incognito, then neither the Jews that sought to kill him would recognize him, and neither would his brethren recognize him since he just finished telling them that he wasn't going up to the feast. I'm not the ultimate judge on what exactly constitutes lying. But the scripture reference in John 7:1-10 contains what closely resembles a lie to me, or at least some sneaky deceptive behavior. If John 7:1-10 does record an account of Jesus telling a lie, then I don't believe it. Jesus had no need to lie or to disguise himself. Jesus had no problem causing whomever he didn't want to see him not to see him, as is evidenced in the following scripture reference.

John 8:57-59
Then said the Jews unto him, Thou art not yet fifty years old, and hast thou seen Abraham? Jesus said unto them, Verily, verily, I say unto you, Before Abraham was, I am. **Then took they up stones to cast at him: but Jesus hid himself and went out of the temple, going through the midst of them, and so passed by.**

As is demonstrated in John 8:57-59, Jesus had no reason to lie or to go anywhere incognito. After all, Jesus is the Son of God. Jesus could perform miracles at will. The New Testament scriptures are replete with the miracles of Jesus. When I look at John 8:57-59 where Jesus went right through the midst of his enemies that had taken up stones to cast at him, then I'm not going to believe in John 7:1-10 where John writes that Jesus said one thing to the brethren and then did the opposite. It is not in Jesus' nature to lie, or to be sneaky and deceptive. What I am doing is laying it out before you, but it's up to you to look it up in your own Bible, then pray and meditate with God about it, and ask God to send his Holy Spirit to guide you in the truth, (as in John 16:13 and 1 John 4:1-6) before you make up your mind if Jesus lied to the brethren in John 7:1-10, or is this another case of interpolation in today's Bible.

Chapter 43 - Glaringly Apparent Genealogical Error

THE NEXT SCRIPTURE references that I want to point out to you as flawed are going to be a little more difficult for me to lay out because we are dealing with genealogies again. The last time I pointed out genealogy errors, it had to do with who fathered whom, and who was whose grandson. In the following Bible error of Matthew 1:1-17, I will follow the scripture text in my King James Bible exactly as it is written, but instead of writing it horizontally on the page, I will list the genealogies vertically so that it will be easier for me to number each generation, thus making it possible to keep track of the number of generations in a glance.

Matthew 1:1-17

The book of the generation of Jesus Christ, the son of David, the son of Abraham.

1. **Abraham**
2. **Abraham begat Isaac**
3. Isaac begat Jacob
4. Jacob begat Judas
5. Judas begat Phares

6. Phares begat Esrom
7. Esrom begat Aram
8. Aram begat Aminadab
9. Aminadab begat Naasson
10. Naasson begat Salmon
11. Salmon begat Booz
12. Booz begat Obed
13. Obed begat Jesse
14. Jesse begat David
15. David begat Solomon
16. Solomon begat Roboam
17. Roboam begat Abia
18. Abia begat Asa
19. Asa begat Josaphat
20. Josaphat begat Joram
21. Joram begat Ozias
22. Ozias begat Joatham
23. Joatham begat Achaz
24. Achaz begat Ezekias
25. Ezekias begat Manasses
26. Manasses begat Amon
27. Amon begat Josias
28. Josias begat Jechonias (and his brethren, about the time they were carried away to Babylon)
29. Jechonias begat Salathiel
30. Salathiel begat Zorobabel
31. Zorobabel begat Abiud
32. Abiud begat Eliakim
33. Eliakim begat Azor
34. Azor begat Sadoc
35. Sadoc begat Achim
36. Achim begat Eliud
37. Eliud begat Eleazar
38. Eleazar begat Matthan
39. Matthan begat Jacob

40. Jacob begat Joseph
41. Joseph, the husband of Mary, of whom was born **Jesus**, who is called Christ
42. Jesus

So all the generations from Abraham to David are fourteen generations; and from David until the carrying away into Babylon are fourteen generations; and from the carrying away into Babylon unto Christ are fourteen generations.

The next scripture reference that I want to point out, to compare with the last scripture reference of Matthew 1:1-17, is Luke 3:23-34. In Luke 3:23-34, Luke also lists the genealogies, but he does it backwards from Matthew's listing. Matthew's listing started with Abraham and ended with Jesus. Luke's listing starts with Jesus, and lists all the way back to Adam and Eve. But for the purposes of this demonstration I will end with Abraham.

Luke 3:23-34

1. Joseph
2. Jesus was the son of Joseph
3. Joseph was the son of Heli
4. Heli was the son of Matthat
5. Matthat was the son of Levi
6. Levi was the son of Melchi
7. Melchi was the son of Janna
8. Janna was the son of Joseph
9. Joseph was the son of Mattathias
10. Mattathias was the son of Amos
11. Amos was the son of Naum
12. Naum was the son of Esli
13. Esli was the son of Nagge
14. Nagge was the son of Maath
15. Maath was the son of Mattathias
16. Mattathias was the son of Semei

17. Semei was the son of Joseph
18. Joseph was the son of Juda
19. Juda was the son of Joanna
20. Joanna was the son of Rhesa
21. Rhesa was the son of Zorobabel
22. Zorobabel was the son of Salathiel
23. Salathiel was the son of Neri
24. Neri was the son of Melchi
25. Melchi was the son of Addi
26. Addi was the son of Cosam
27. Cosam was the son of Elmodam
28. Elmodam was the son of Er.
29. Er was the son of Jose
30. Jose was the son of Eliezer
31. Eliezer was the son of Jorim
32. Jorim was the son of Matthat
33. Matthat was the son of Levi
34. Levi was the son of Simeon
35. Simeon was the son of Juda
36. Juda was the son of Joseph
37. Joseph was the son of Jonan
38. Jonan was the son of Eliakim
39. Eliakim was the son of Melea
40. Melea was the son of Menan
41. Menan was the son of Mattatha
42. Mattatha was the son of Nathan
43. Nathan was the son of David
44. David was the son of Jesse
45. Jesse was the son of Obed
46. Obed was the son of Booz
47. Booz was the son of Salmon
48. Salmon was the son of Naasson
49. Naasson was the son of Aminadab
50. Aminadab was the son of Aram
51. Aram was the son of Esrom

52. Esrom was the son of Phares
53. Phares was the son of Juda
54. Juda was the son of Jacob
55. Jacob was the son of Isaac
56. Isaac was the son of Abraham
57. Abraham

Now that I have laid it out for you vertically with a numbering system, it is easy to see that something is wrong. In Matthew 1:1-17 we number forty-two generations from Abraham to Jesus. But in Luke 3:23-34 we number fifty-seven generations from Jesus to Abraham. It should not matter if the Gospel authors listed the generations from Abraham to Jesus, or from Jesus to Abraham. Either way, if there was not an error in the Bible, they should total the same number. They do not total the same number. They differ by fifteen generations. Therefore here is one more proof that there are flaws and errors in today's Bible. I will not blame God for it. Heaven forbid! When God divinely inspired a human being to write something down, God made sure that it was correct as originally written down under the power and inspiration of God's Holy Spirit. Let's read on and I will point out more scripture references that I have a problem with from today's Bible.

Chapter 44 - What Was the Sign of Who Would Betray Jesus

Compare Matthew 26:20-23
Now when the even was come, he sat down with the twelve. And as they did eat, he said, Verily I say unto you, that one of you shall betray me. And they were exceeding sorrowful, and began every one of them to say unto him, Lord, is it I? **And he answered and said, He that dippeth his hand with me in the dish, the same shall betray me.**

With John 13:21-26
When Jesus had thus said, he was troubled in spirit, and testified, and said, Verily, verily, I say unto you, that one of you shall betray me. Then the disciples looked one on another, doubting of whom he spake. Now there was leaning on Jesus' bosom one of his disciples, whom Jesus loved. Simon Peter therefore beckoned to him, that he should ask who it should be of whom he spake. He then lying on Jesus' breast saith unto him, Lord, who is it? **Jesus answered, He it is, to whom I shall give a sop, when I have dipped it. And when he had dipped the sop, he gave it to Judas Iscariot, the son of Simon.**

WELL, WHICH ONE is right? In Matthew 26:20-23 we see Jesus answering by saying that whomever dips their bread in the dipping broth at the same time as Jesus is, that is the one who will betray him. But in John 13:21-26 we see Jesus answering by saying that whomever he shall give a sopped piece of bread to, that is the one who will betray him. Both accounts cannot be right because they are too different. Either one may be the correct one, but they both can't be correct. So by process of elimination, whichever account is indeed right, then the other account has to be wrong. This is just one more proof to reinforce and support my claim that today's Bible has been tampered with from when God's Holy Spirit divinely inspired the original writers. Let's read on and I will point out another scripture reference that I have a problem with in today's Bible.

Chapter 45 - Who Instructed the Disciples to Carry Weapons

Compare Matthew 26:50-55
And Jesus said unto him, Friend, wherefore art thou come? Then came they, and laid hands on Jesus, and took him. And, behold, **one of them which were with Jesus stretched out his hand, and drew his sword, and struck a servant of the high priest's, and smote off his ear. Then said Jesus unto him, Put up again thy sword into his place: <u>for all they that take the sword shall perish with the sword.</u>** Thinkest thou that I cannot now pray to my Father, and he shall presently give me more than twelve legions of angels? But how then shall the scriptures be fulfilled, that thus it must be? In that same hour said Jesus to the multitudes, Are ye come out as against a thief with swords and staves for to take me? I sat daily with you teaching in the temple, and ye laid no hold on me.

And Luke 22:48-53
But Jesus said unto him, Judas, betrayest thou the Son of man with a kiss? When they which were about him saw what would follow, **they said unto him, Lord, shall we smite with the sword? And one of them smote the servant of the high priest,**

and cut off his right ear. And Jesus answered and said, Suffer ye thus far. And he touched his ear, and healed him. Then Jesus said unto the chief priests, and captains of the temple, and the elders, which were come to him, Be ye come out, as against a thief, with swords and staves? When I was daily with you in the temple, ye stretched forth no hands against me: but this is your hour, and the power of darkness.

<u>With Luke 22:35-38</u>
And he said unto them, When I sent you without purse, and scrip, and shoes, lacked ye any thing? And they said, Nothing. **Then said he unto them, But now, he that hath a purse, let him take it, and likewise his scrip: and he that hath no sword, let him sell his garment, and buy one.** For I say unto you, that this that is written must yet be accomplished in me, And he was reckoned among the transgressors: for the things concerning me have an end. **And they said, Lord, behold, here are two swords. And he said unto them, It is enough.**

I HAVE INCLUDED the three scripture references above to point out who gave the order to supply themselves with arms. Most clergy seem to only tell us about the story in Matthew 26:50-55 and Luke 22:48-53, about one of the disciples jumping up and cutting off the ear from one of the high priest's servants that came to apprehend Jesus. I am guessing there are a lot of readers out there who haven't been told by their clergy that it was Jesus himself, as described in Luke 22:35-38, that gave the order for them to be armed. That is confusing compared to what Jesus said in Matthew 26:50-55, "For all they that take the sword shall perish with the sword." It is also confusing when we look at what Jesus taught in Matthew 5:39.

<u>Matthew 5:39</u>
But I say unto you, That ye resist not evil: but whosoever shall smite thee on thy right cheek, turn to him the other also.

This causes me to wonder what exactly is going on with the accounts of one of Jesus' disciples cutting off one of the high priest's servant's ears. And I am equally puzzled about why in Luke 22:35-38, it was Jesus himself who instructed them to carry weapons in the first place. At this point in time I do not draw any conclusions for you. I merely put it forward for you to ponder and draw your own conclusions about what is going on with the above four scripture references. They seem confusing and contradicting when you take them in total and examine them.

Chapter 46 - Was Jesus Really Betrayed by a Kiss

<u>Compare Matthew 26:47-50</u>
And while he yet spake, lo, Judas, one of the twelve, came, and with him a great multitude with swords and staves, from the chief priests and elders of the people. **Now he that betrayed him gave them a sign, saying, Whomsoever I shall kiss, that same is he: hold him fast. And forthwith he came to Jesus, and said, Hail, master, and kissed him.** And Jesus said unto him, Friend, wherefore art thou come? Then came they, and laid hands on Jesus, and took him.

<u>With John 18:3-9</u>
Judas then, having received a band of men and officers from the chief priests and Pharisees, cometh thither with lanterns and torches and weapons. **Jesus therefore, knowing all things that should come upon him, went forth, and said unto them, Whom seek ye? They answered him, Jesus of Nazareth. Jesus saith unto them, I am he. And Judas also, which betrayed him, stood with them.** As soon then as he had said unto them, I am he, they went backward, and fell to the ground. Then he asked them again, Whom seek ye? **And they said, Jesus of Nazareth. Jesus**

answered, I have told you that I am he: if therefore ye seek me, let these go their way: That the saying might be fulfilled, which he spake, Of them which thou gavest me have I lost none.

THESE ARE TWO different Gospel accounts of the same incident. In Matthew 26:47-50, we see that Judas betrayed Jesus with a kiss to show the chief priests which person was Jesus. But in John 18:3-9, there is no kiss of betrayal described. It seems that in John's account it was Jesus who took the initiative, went forward and approached the mob, asking them who they were looking for. When they said they were looking for Jesus, he answered them "I am he." In John's account Judas was only standing with the mob. Not only does John's account not mention anything about a kiss, but he goes on to point out that when Jesus told the mob that he was Jesus, the power of his authority and Godhood caused the mob to fall backward on the ground. I don't know which account to believe. But when you compare the accounts side by side, it is apparent that they differ. This is just one more instance that makes me suspicious as to whether there isn't some form of interpolation involved. Some of the scripture references that I have quoted in this book are obviously in error, while others are suspect. If there weren't the glaringly apparent flaws and errors in today's Bible, I wouldn't be suspicious of the less obvious problematic accounts. I have presented the above scripture references for you to ponder about and pray over, and then make up your own mind one way or the other. Following are more scripture references that I have a problem with.

Chapter 47 - Did Somebody Really Help Jesus Carry His Cross

<u>Compare Matthew 27:31-33</u>
And after that they had mocked him, they took the robe off from him, and put his own raiment on him, and led him away to crucify him. **And as they came out, they found a man of Cyrene, Simon by name: him they compelled to bear his cross.** And when they were come unto a place called Golgotha, that is to say, a place of a skull.

<u>With John 19:16-17</u>
Then delivered he him therefore unto them to be crucified. **And they took Jesus, and led him away. And he bearing his cross forth into a place called the place of a skull,** which is called in the Hebrew Golgotha:

WELL, WHICH ONE is right? They both can't be right. Did a man of Cyrene, Simon by name, carry Jesus' cross for him to Golgotha? That is what the Matthew 27:31-33 account says. Or did Jesus bear his own cross to Golgotha? That is what the John 19:16-17 account says. In any event, regardless which one is right, I don't believe it was God that caused this confusion. God wouldn't cause the Holy Spirit to divinely inspire confusion. The above is one more proof that leads me to believe that today's Bible has been tampered with and interpolated. Let's read on and I will point out another scripture reference that I have a problem with.

Chapter 48 - How Many Really Died in One Day

<u>Compare Numbers 25:1-9</u>
And Israel abode in Shittim, and the people began to commit whoredom with the daughters of Moab. And they called the people unto the sacrifices of their gods: and the people did eat, and bowed down to their gods. And Israel joined himself unto Baalpeor and the anger of the Lord was kindled against Israel. And the Lord said unto Moses, Take all the heads of the people, and hang them up before the Lord against the sun, that the fierce anger of the Lord may be turned away from Israel. And Moses said unto the judges of Israel, Slay ye every one of his men that were joined unto Baalpeor. And, behold, one of the children of Israel came and brought unto his brethren a Midianitish woman in the sight of Moses, and in the sight of all the congregation of the children of Israel, who were weeping before the door of the tabernacle of the congregation. And when Phinehas, the son of Eleazar, the son of Aaron the priest, saw it, he rose up from among the congregation, and took a javelin in his hand; And he went after the man of Israel into the tent, and thrust both of them through, the man of Israel, and the woman through her belly. So

the plague was stayed from the children of Israel. **And those that died in the plague were twenty and four thousand.**

With 1 Corinthians 10:1-8

Moreover, brethren, I would not that ye should be ignorant, how that all our fathers were under the cloud, and all passed through the sea; And were all baptized unto Moses in the cloud and in the sea; And did all eat the same spiritual meat; And did all drink the same spiritual drink: for they drank of that spiritual Rock that followed them: and that Rock was Christ. But with many of them God was not well pleased: for they were overthrown in the wilderness. Now these things were our examples, to the intent we should not lust after evil things, as they also lusted. Neither be ye idolaters, as were some of them; as it is written, The people sat down to eat and drink, and rose up to play. Neither let us commit fornication, as some of them committed, **and fell in one day three and twenty thousand.**

IN NUMBERS 25:1-9 is the account of Moses and the people he led out of Egypt, with whom he wandered forty years in the desert, and the sins the people of Israel committed during their journey. God had been good to them. God led them by day in a pillar of cloud, and by night in a pillar of fire. God miraculously fed them every day. But some of the people joined themselves to Baalpeor, and fornicated and ate and drank, and lusted after evil things. This same account is summarized in 1 Corinthians 10:1-8. However, if you will especially notice the part that I highlighted in bold, you will see that the Numbers 25:1-9 account says those that died were twenty four thousand, while the 1 Corinthians 10:1-8 account says that twenty three thousand died.

Well, which one is right? Was it twenty four thousand that died? Or was it twenty three thousand that died? If one of the accounts is right, then the other account, by process of elimination, has to be wrong. Let's read on and I will point out another scripture reference in today's Bible that I have a problem with.

Chapter 49 - What Did the Men With Saul Actually See and/or Hear

<u>Compare Acts 9:3-8</u>
And as he journeyed, he came near Damascus: and suddenly there shined round about him a light from heaven: And he fell to the earth, and heard a voice saying unto him, Saul, Saul, why persecutest thou me? And he said, Who art thou, Lord? And the Lord said, I am Jesus whom thou persecutest: it is hard for thee to kick against the pricks. And he trembling and astonished said, Lord, what wilt thou have me to do? And the Lord said unto him, Arise, and go into the city, and it shall be told thee what thou must do. **And the men which journeyed with him stood speechless, hearing a voice, but seeing no man.** And Saul arose from the earth; and when his eyes were opened, he saw no man: but they led him by the hand, and brought him into Damascus.

<u>With Acts 22:6-11</u>
And it came to pass, that, as I made my journey, and was come nigh unto Damascus about noon, suddenly there shone from heaven a great light round about me. And I fell unto the ground, and heard a voice saying unto me, Saul, Saul, why persecutest thou me? And I answered, Who art thou, Lord? And he said unto me,

I am Jesus of Nazareth, whom thou persecutest. **And they that were with me saw indeed the light, and were afraid; but they heard not the voice of him that spake to me.** And I said, What shall I do, Lord? And the Lord said unto me, Arise, and go into Damascus; and there it shall be told thee of all things which are appointed for thee to do. And when I could not see for the glory of that light, being led by the hand of them that were with me, I came to Damascus.

And Acts 26:13-19
At Midday, O king, I saw in the way a light from heaven, above the brightness of the sun, shining round about me and them which journeyed with me. And when we were all fallen to the earth, **I heard a voice speaking unto me,** and saying in the Hebrew tongue, Saul, Saul, why persecutest thou me? it is hard for thee to kick against the pricks. And I said, Who art thou, Lord? And he said, I am Jesus whom thou persecutest. But rise, and stand upon thy feet: for I have appeared unto thee for this purpose, to make thee a minister and a witness both of these things which thou hast seen, and of those things in the which I will appear unto thee; Delivering thee from the people, and from the Gentiles, unto whom now I send thee. To open their eyes, and to turn them from darkness to light, and from the power of Satan unto God, that they may receive forgiveness of sins, and inheritance among them which are sanctified by faith that is in me. Whereupon, 0 king Agrippa, I was not disobedient unto the heavenly vision:

THE ABOVE THREE scripture references all tell the account of Saul seeing Jesus appear to him on the road to Damascus. However, there are flaws and errors that are glaringly apparent when you closely examine them and compare one with the other. I did not highlight in bold all of the flaws and errors. I thought that would be too confusing. So I highlighted only one error, but I will tell you the other errors that I find in these three scripture references.

Looking at the part I highlighted in Acts 9:3-8, we see that the men that journeyed with Saul heard a voice, but saw no man. In the highlighted part in Acts 22:6-11, we see that the men that journeyed with Saul heard not the voice. And in Acts 26:13-19 Saul says he heard the voice and doesn't indicate one way or the other whether the men with him heard the voice. All three accounts cannot be right. Between Acts 9:3-8, and Acts 22:6-11, the men that accompanied Saul either did hear the voice or they did not hear the voice. Whichever one of those accounts is right, then by process of elimination, the other account is wrong. This is one error that is glaringly apparent. It doesn't take any wondering, or suspicion. It is clearly an error in today's Bible.

To illustrate another problem I have with the above three scripture references from Acts, look at Acts 9:3-8. In the sentence just before the bold highlight, you will see that it says, "And the Lord said unto him, Arise, and go into the city, and it shall be told thee what thou must do." If you look at Acts 22:6-11, in the sentences just after the bold highlight, you will see that it says, "And I said, What shall I do, Lord? And the Lord said unto me, Arise, and go into Damascus; and there it shall be told thee of all things which are appointed for thee to do." Both of those scripture references from Acts 9:3-8 and Acts 22:6-11 agree with each other as to what the Lord told Saul to do. Both scripture references have the Lord telling Saul to go to Damascus and <u>then</u> he would be told what he must do. However, when you look at the same account in Acts 26: 13-19, you will see that the Lord tells Saul right then and there what he wants Saul to do. In Acts 26:13-19, it shows that Saul did not have to go to Damascus to be told what to do. The following scripture reference is what happened in that account.

<u>Acts 26:16-18</u>
But rise, and stand upon thy feet: for I have appeared unto thee for this purpose, to make thee a minister and a witness both of these things which thou hast seen, and of those things in the which I will appear unto thee; Delivering thee from the people,

and from the Gentiles, unto whom now I send thee, To open their eyes, and to turn them from darkness to light, and from the power of Satan unto God, that they may receive forgiveness of sins, and inheritance among them which are sanctified by faith that is in me.

When I compare the accounts in Acts 9:3-8 and Acts 22:6-11, against the account in Acts 26:16-18 quoted above, it is glaringly apparent that there is another error. Either Jesus told Saul on the road to Damascus or, the Lord told Saul to go to Damascus first and then it will be told to him what he must do. It cannot be both. It is either one or the other. Now there are two errors that are glaringly apparent in the above scripture references in today's Bible.

For yet another problem I have with the above three scripture references from Acts, look at Acts 9:3-8, where it says, "And he fell to the earth,…" If you look at Acts 22:6-11 you will see where it says, "And I fell unto the ground,…." Both of those scripture references from Acts 9:3-8 and Acts 22:6-11 agree with each other by saying that Saul fell to the ground when the Lord met Saul on the road to Damascus. However, when you look at the same account in Acts 26:13-19, you will see a different account of what took place. The following scripture reference is what happened in that account.

Acts 26:13-14

At Midday, O king, I saw in the way a light from heaven, above the brightness of the sun, **shining round about me and them which journeyed with me. And when we were all fallen to the earth,** I heard a voice speaking unto me, and saying in the Hebrew tongue, Saul, Saul, why persecutest thou me? It is hard for thee to kick against the pricks.

Well, which one was it? Was it Saul who fell to the ground? In Acts 22:6-11 Saul, now Paul, said in verse 7, "I" fell unto the ground. But in Acts 26:13-14 he is saying they all fell to the ground. I don't know which account is the right one, because it is too confusing to be certain. And this is the third error that I find in the above scriptures. I cannot, or will not, blame God for the confusion in these scripture references because God is not the author of confusion.

God would not divinely inspire the same account to be written down in different ways in different places in the Bible. These errors I add to the body of evidence that I have found that leads me to believe that today's Bible has been tampered with and is interpolated. Now I will point out other scripture references that I have a problem with in today's Bible.

Chapter 50 - How Many Kindred/ Souls Were in the House of Jacob

Compare Genesis 46:27
And the sons of Joseph, which were born him in Egypt, were two souls: **all the souls of the house of Jacob, which came into Egypt, were threescore and ten.**

With Acts 7:14
Then sent Joseph, and called his father Jacob to him, **and all his kindred, threescore and fifteen souls.**

WELL, WHICH ONE is right? Since each of the scripture references about Joseph and all his people have a different number quoted, they both cannot be right. The Genesis 46:27 account says the number of souls are seventy (since a score is twenty). In the Acts 7:14 account, it says the number of souls are seventy five. In the Genesis 46:27 account, even if you added the total souls that were born to Joseph to the final tally, it would still only add up to seventy two. Yet according to Acts 7:14 the count adds up to seventy five. Genesis 46:27 does not add up to the seventy five souls that are claimed to be the number of souls of Joseph and his kindred in the Acts 7:14 account of seventy five. Clearly this is another glaringly apparent error in today's Bible. It has to be the fault of human tampering because God is not the author of confusion. God did not divinely inspire it to be written down differently in two different parts of the Bible. Therefore this is one more proof that today's Bible has been tampered with and is interpolated from the original divinely inspired Bible that God dictated to the original Bible writers to write down in the Bible. Let's read on and I will point out other scripture references that I have a problem with in today's Bible.

Chapter 51 - How Many Days Was Jesus in the Grave

IN THE NEXT set of scripture references from the Bible that I will quote and compare, we deal with the topic of the number of days that Jesus was dead before he rose from the grave on Sunday morning. For clarity, and to help the reader follow along as it progresses, I will insert notes in parenthesis to denote which day we are talking about, as in (died Friday evening), (the next day is Saturday), and (Sunday morning). Of course what I enclose in parenthesis is not part of the scripture reference, but is only an aid to help you track the timeline with me.

Compare Matthew 12:38-40
Then certain of the scribes and of the Pharisees answered, saying, Master, we would see a sign from thee. But he answered and said unto them, An evil and adulterous generation seeketh after a sign; **and there shall no sign be given to it, but the sign of the prophet Jonas: For as Jonas was three days and three nights in the whale's belly; so shall the Son of man be three days and three nights in the heart of the earth.**

<u>With Matthew 27:45-28:6</u>
Now from the sixth hour there was darkness over all the land
unto the ninth hour. And about the ninth hour Jesus cried with
a loud voice, saying, Eli, Eli, lama sabachthani? that is to say, My
God, my God, why hast thou forsaken me? Some of them that
stood there, when they heard that, said, This man calleth for Elias.
And straightway one of them ran, and took a spunge, and filled
it with vinegar, and put it on a reed, and gave him to drink. The
rest said, Let be, let us see whether Elias will come to save him.
**Jesus, when he had cried again with a loud voice, yielded up
the ghost.** (Jesus died on Friday evening.) And, behold, the veil of
the temple was rent in twain from the top to the bottom; and the
earth did quake, and the rocks rent; And the graves were opened;
and many bodies of the saints which slept arose, And came out
of the graves after his resurrection, and went into the holy city,
and appeared unto many. Now when the centurion, and they that
were with him, watching Jesus, saw the earthquake, and those
things that were done, they feared greatly, saying, Truly this was
the Son of God. And many women were there beholding afar off,
which followed Jesus from Galilee, ministering unto him: Among
which was Mary Magdalene, and Mary the mother of James and
Joses, and the mother of Zebedee's children. When the even was
come, there came a rich man of Arimathaea, named Joseph, who
also himself was Jesus' disciple: He went to Pilate, and begged the
body of Jesus. Then Pilate commanded the body to be delivered.
And when Joseph had taken the body, he wrapped it in a clean
linen cloth, And laid it in his own new tomb, which he had hewn
out in the rock: and he rolled a great stone to the door of the
sepulchre, and departed. And there was Mary Magdalene, and
the other Mary, sitting over against the sepulchre. **Now the next
day,** (the next day after Good Friday is Saturday) that followed
the day of the preparation, the chief priests and Pharisees came
together unto Pilate, Saying, Sir, we remember that that deceiver
said, while he was yet alive, After three days I will rise again.
Command therefore that the sepulchre be made sure until the

third day, lest his disciples come by night, and steal him away, and say unto the people, He is risen from the dead: so the last error shall be worse than the first. Pilate said unto them, Ye have a watch: go your way, make it as sure as ye can. So they went, and made the sepulchre sure, sealing the stone, and setting a watch. **In the end of the sabbath, as it began to dawn toward the first day of the week,** (Easter Sunday morning) **came Mary Magdalene and the other Mary to see the sepulchre.** And, behold, there was a great earthquake: for the angel of the Lord descended from heaven, and came and rolled back the stone from the door, and sat upon it. His countenance was like lightning, and his raiment white as snow: And for fear of him the keepers did shake, and became as dead men. And the angel answered and said unto the women, Fear not ye: for I know that ye seek Jesus, which was crucified. He is not here: for he is risen, as he said. Come, see the place where the Lord lay.

Now when we add up the time Jesus spent in the grave, from Good Friday evening, through the day after Good Friday, which is Saturday, up until early Easter Sunday when Mary Magdalene and the other Mary arrived at dawn at Jesus' tomb and found he had risen, it is two nights and one full day in the grave. Even if we add the day of the crucifixion, Good Friday, before we count Good Friday evening, it still only adds up to two days and two nights in the grave. If Jesus spent two nights and one day, or two nights and two days in the grave, then the Matthew 12:38-40 scripture reference is wrong, where Jesus said the only sign would be the Son of man being three days and three nights in the earth. However, if the Matthew 12:38-40 scripture reference is right, then Matthew 27:45-28:6 is wrong. Any way we add it up, one or the other has to be wrong. They can't both be accurate. Therefore, here is another proof that today's Bible has flaws and errors in it and has been interpolated.

Chapter 52 - Can Works Get Us Saved and Into Heaven

NOW I WILL give you one more selection from today's Bible that I have a problem with. It was hard for me to accept what I found in the following three scripture references, because when they are examined together side by side, something leapt out at me that went against my deep Christian faith. You may experience the same thing. If you will remember in the beginning of my book I talked about how I had to work through the classic five stages of grief, you will now better understand what I meant when I said that. Well the aggregate body of what I found out over decades of Bible study was enough of a shock to me in itself, but what the next three scripture references intimate was especially hard for me to understand and accept. It took me a while to get where I am, which is at peace with all this.

Compare Mark 16:15-19
And he said unto them, Go ye into all the world, and preach the gospel to every creature. **He that <u>believeth</u> and is baptized shall be saved;** but he that believeth not shall be damned. And these signs shall follow them that believe; In my name shall they cast out devils; they shall speak with new tongues; They shall take

up serpents; and if they drink any deadly thing, it shall not hurt them; they shall lay hands on the sick, and they shall recover. So then after the Lord had spoken unto them, he was received up into heaven, and sat on the right hand of God.

<u>And Romans 10:9-10</u>
That if thou shalt confess with thy mouth the Lord Jesus, and shalt <u>believe</u> in thine heart that God hath raised him from the dead, thou shalt be saved. For with the heart man <u>believeth</u> unto righteousness; and with the mouth confession is made unto salvation.

<u>With Matthew 7:21-24</u>
Not every one that saith unto me, Lord, Lord, shall enter into the kingdom of heaven; **but he that <u>doeth</u> the will of my Father which is in heaven.** Many will say to me in that day, Lord, Lord, have we not prophesied in thy name? and in thy name have cast out devils? and in thy name done many wonderful works? And then will I profess unto them, I never knew you: depart from me, ye that work iniquity. Therefore whosoever heareth these sayings of mine, and **<u>doeth</u>** them, I will liken him unto a wise man, which built his house upon a rock.

<u>James 2:17</u>
Even so faith, if it hath not works, is dead, being alone.

When we look at Mark 16:15-19, we see that we can be saved through our "belief." In Romans 10:9-10, we see that we can be saved through our "belief." This is what I have been taught all of my life. This is what I still believe today. There is no getting around it: if we do as the key scripture reference says in Romans 10:9-10, we are saved (Born Again) and will not go to hell. Of course, after I invited Jesus to come into my heart and be my personal Lord and Savior over two decades ago, I started to change my thoughts and behavior. I had a new desire inside of me. I desired to please God and live by Godly standards. Slowly but surely, by little baby steps, the change, from an unsaved infidel to a man that lives to serve God as best as he can, transpired. This is where I am today. The process never ends in this life. I am continually changing, one little baby step at a time, hopefully for the better. I know that heaven is my eternal reward after I pass from this life. I know it because Jesus died and paid the price for my sin. He did that for me. I appropriate Jesus' shed blood for me, by intentionally doing what it says in Romans 10:9-10. My belief in Jesus and his blood shed for me, is what assures me of my salvation. But when we compare that with what Jesus is saying in Matthew 7:21-24, that calling on him is not good enough, it just doesn't add up. In Matthew 7:21-24, Jesus is saying it will take doing works in order to get to heaven. That scripture reference runs counter to everything I've learned through my Christian journey. Matthew 7:21-24 is very confusing to me, when compared to Mark 16:15-19 and Romans 10:9-10.

There is only one way a Christian can lose his salvation, as it says in the scripture reference of Mark 3: 28-29.

Mark 3:28-29
Verily I say unto you, **All** sins shall be forgiven unto the sons of men, and blasphemies wherewith soever they shall blaspheme: But he that shall blaspheme against the Holy Ghost hath never forgiveness, but is in danger of eternal damnation:

That is a most serious warning from God concerning those that blaspheme against the Holy Ghost. ALL other sins will be forgiven. What exactly is blaspheming against the Holy Ghost? I believe that is when a Christian renounces his salvation that he proclaimed by accepting Jesus Christ as Lord. Getting back to our discussion about Matthew 7:21-24 where Jesus is supposed to have said that when it is time for some who have prophesied, cast out devils in Jesus' name, and done many wonderful works to enter into heaven, Jesus will say he never knew them. It just doesn't add up. The only way anyone can prophecy, cast out devils in Jesus' name, and do many wonderful works, is if they know and believe in Jesus. If you don't think so, just let a non-believer try being a prophet of God, casting out devils, and doing many wonderful works and see what happens. Jesus knows who believes in him and who the heavenly Father is blessing. In that same scripture reference Jesus is supposed to have said that it takes <u>doing</u> to get into the kingdom of heaven, while Mark 16:15-16 and Romans 10:9-10 both say that it only takes <u>believing</u> to get into heaven. If the people in Matthew 7:21-24 are saying Lord, Lord, then they are believing on the Lord and calling on his name. Anyone who calls on the name of the Lord shall in no wise be cast out.

<u>Romans 10:13-14a</u>
For **whosoever** shall call upon the name of the Lord **shall** be saved. How then shall they call on him in whom they have not believed?

<u>John 6:37</u>
All that the Father giveth me shall come to me; and him that cometh to me I will in no wise cast out.

There is no way that by doing good works anyone can earn their way into heaven. This is clearly pointed out in the following scripture reference.

<u>Ephesians 2:8-9</u>
For by grace are ye saved through faith; and that not of yourselves: it is the gift of God: **Not of works,** lest any man should boast.

Apparently the people Jesus was talking to in Matthew 7:21-24 believed enough in Jesus that they were able to cast out devils in Jesus' name. They prophesied and did many wonderful works. They combined their faith with their good works in Jesus' name. To my understanding, a person cannot do that and be in unbelief. A person who does all those things has to believe. Jesus himself says in Mark 16:15-19 that the signs of them that believe are casting out devils, speaking with new tongues, taking up serpents;

and if they drink any deadly thing, it shall not hurt them; they shall lay hands on the sick, and they shall recover. When you believe in Jesus, then the signs mentioned in Mark 16:15-19 are what God will bless you with. Today, I know some very wonderful Christians who lay hands on sick people and pray for them to be healed. I pray for others to be healed too. However, they don't always get healed. Success for accomplishing a healing is sporadic. I trust God knows why that is and that is sufficient for me. I do know that according to Matthew 8:16b Jesus healed <u>ALL</u> that were sick. I also believe that today God heals <u>ALL</u> who ask for healing and are prayed for in Jesus' name today. If the healing is not manifested in the person's body today, it is not God's fault. Back in Jesus' day, whomever he was talking to in Matthew 7:21-24 were having their prayer requests blessed by God, because Jesus says they will come to him at the judgment and say, "Have we not prophesied in thy name? and in thy name have cast out devils? and in thy name done many wonderful works?" So if God was blessing those people's prayer requests back in Jesus' day, then why would Jesus say he <u>never</u> knew them? I believe he knew whose prayer requests God the Father was blessing. I and the good Christian men and women of God that I know today believe that we will go to heaven after we die. We have some works, but we are not perfect, (especially me). When I die I don't want justice; I want mercy. I want the mercy that the shed blood of Jesus gives me and the blessed assurance that being in the precious shed blood of Jesus gives me. As good as I try to be, I cannot do enough "works" to earn my way into heaven. Therefore, I present to you the scripture references of Mark 16:15-19, Romans 10:9-10 and Matthew 7:21-24 to demonstrate why I have a serious problem with Matthew 7:21-24. Now that I have presented it to you, it's up to you to check it out in your own Bible, pray and meditate with God about it, and ask God to touch your spirit with his Holy Spirit, to guide you into the truth on what you ultimately decide to think and believe about Matthew 7:21-24.

Chapter 53 - I Do Not Parrot the Party Line

I HAVE TO consider that I might have made an error in a couple of the flawed Bible scripture references that I pointed out that I have a problem with. After all, I am only a human being and I make inadvertent mistakes once in a while like everyone else. I try not to. I don't think I did in any of the scripture references that I pointed out to you in my book. I say I may have possibly made an inadvertent error on a couple of them because sure as shooting, in the future after I publish my book, if I have made a mistake, some slick preacher with a high profile will spend an inordinate amount of pulpit time pointing the one or two mistakes out, in an attempt to discredit my entire book in order to try and keep his membership under his control. But I tell you that if only one or two of the errored scripture references are in fact errors in the HOLY BIBLE that we have today, that is all it takes to discredit the entire Bible, and the "party line" that all the ministers, priests, and televangelists have all been telling us from the pulpit Sunday after Sunday, year after year: that the Holy Bible is the infallible, unaltered, unerring Word of God. I've heard them say that if there is one mistake in the Bible, then you can't believe any of it. They have told us that the Bible is flawless and unerring. So according to what we've been told from the pulpit all these years, it only takes one proven flaw to discredit the entire Bible. Well I don't go that far. I think, even though I have given you the proof that today's Bible has flaws and errors in it and that it has been interpolated, I also believe there is still a lot of it that has not been interpolated. A lot of it still is the divinely inspired Word of God that was written down by holy men of God that spake as they were moved by the Holy Ghost. My book will help guide you around the Bible errors and interpolations that I have found and pointed out to you. I'm not throwing the baby out with the bath water. It's still predominately an account of God's Word to us. It's still the "good book." The main reason I have decided to include this particular paragraph in my book is that in case it turns out that I have made an inadvertent mistake or two, I don't want the lambs of God to be fooled into believing that an inadvertent mistake or two discredits my entire book. It doesn't. Personally, at this point in time I don't believe I have made an inadvertent mistake in any part of my book. I only humbly say that in the future I might find out that I have, because I am only human like anybody else, and we humans do sometimes make inadvertent mistakes. I will close this topic by saying that if only one of the flaws and errors that I have pointed out about today's Bible turn out to be a Bible error, that is all it takes to prove that the Bible is flawed. And I have given you the proof that today's Bible is flawed and has errors in it more than once in my book. And that proves that what we've been told from the pulpit all these years, that the Holy Bible is infallible and doesn't have even one mistake in it, is wrong. I have proven to you the hypothesis for the title of my book that: <u>What We've Been Told About the HOLY BIBLE is a Lie and Here's the Proof</u>.

As I finish writing this book, I want to speak on a few topics, before I close. I hope that after you have checked all the scripture references that I have pointed out to you and prayed and meditated with God about them, that you too will come to the conclusion, as the title of my book says: <u>What We've Been Told About the</u>

HOLY BIBLE is a Lie and Here's the Proof. It will be easy for you to compare what I have pointed out to you with what you have been told from the clergy or church hierarchy at your church. You will know if your clergy has been pointing out all parts of the Bible to you, or choosing selected parts of the Bible to keep you ignorant of the whole truth about today's Bible. If your clergy is a cabal, using the church as their fiefdom, in order to fleece the sheep, then I suggest you get away from them. That type of clergy fits the description spoken by Jesus in the following scripture reference.

Matthew 23:13-27
But woe unto you, scribes and Pharisees, hypocrites! for ye shut up the kingdom of heaven against men: for ye neither go in yourselves, neither suffer ye them that are entering to go in. Woe unto you, scribes and Pharisees, hypocrites! for ye devour widows' houses, and for a pretence make long prayer: therefore ye shall receive the greater damnation. Woe unto you, scribes and Pharisees, hypocrites! for ye compass sea and land to make one proselyte, and when he is made, ye make him twofold more the child of hell than yourselves. Woe unto you, ye blind guides, which say, Whosoever shall swear by the temple, it is nothing; but whosoever shall swear by the gold of the temple, he is a debtor! Ye fools and blind: for whether is greater, the gold, or the temple that sanctifieth the gold? And, Whosoever shall swear by the altar, it is nothing; but whosoever sweareth by the gift that is upon it, he is guilty. Ye fools and blind: for whether is greater, the gift, or the altar that sanctifieth the gift? Whoso therefore shall swear by the altar, sweareth by it, and by all things thereon. And whoso shall swear by the temple, sweareth by it, and by him that dwelleth therein. And he that shall swear by heaven, sweareth by the throne of God, and by him that sitteth thereon. Woe unto you, scribes and Pharisees, hypocrites! for ye pay tithe of mint and anise and cummin, and have omitted the weightier matters of the law, judgment, mercy, and faith: these ought ye to have

done, and not to leave the other undone. Ye blind guides, which strain at a gnat, and swallow a camel. Woe unto you, scribes and Pharisees, hypocrites! for ye make clean the outside of the cup and of the platter, but within they are full of extortion and excess. Thou blind Pharisee, cleanse first that which is within the cup and platter, that the outside of them may be clean also. Woe unto you, scribes and Pharisees, hypocrites! for ye are like unto whited sepulchres, which indeed appear beautiful outward, but are within full of dead men's bones, and of all uncleanness.

There it is. I certainly can't say it any better than Jesus said it. My heart goes out to the laity, the sheep and lambs of God that genuinely and sincerely love God and want to serve him. It is to you folks, the rank and file everyday Christians who fill up the pews every Sunday, that my book is dedicated to. With all my heart I pray in the name of Jesus that God's Holy Spirit touches your heart in a special way, so that by reading my book you will be led to the truth about today's Bible and how today's clergy have withheld that truth from you.

Chapter 54 - The Creator Knows Everything Before We Discover It

BEFORE I CLOSE, I also want to point out some scripture references that are not in error. Considering how many thousands of years ago these were divinely inspired by God to be written down, it just confirms my resolve that God Almighty, the designer and creator of the universe and everything that is in it, is real. After I share the next three scripture references with you, I hope that you will see what I mean.

Psalm 8:8
The fowl of the air, and the fish of the sea, and whatsoever passeth through **the paths of the seas.**

Psalm 8:8 was written a long time before men knew there were continents beyond the Mediterranean and areas that constituted the known world. My point is that there was no transcontinental ocean travel back then. But today we know that there are definite "paths of the sea" used by ocean going vessels. I see the term "the paths of the seas" as God's Holy Spirit giving divine inspiration about God's creation to the writers of the Bible, long before the oceans and "the paths of the seas" were discovered. The next scripture reference is another evidence of God's divine inspiration to the original Bible writers.

Job 26:7
He stretcheth out the north over the empty space, and hangeth the earth upon nothing.

Before the discoveries of more modern science, it was believed that the earth was flat and lay upon a huge support. When Magellan sailed around the earth he discovered that there was nothing visible that supported the earth. However, thousands of years earlier, before Magellan, God divinely inspired it to be written down in Job 26:7 that he had "...hung the earth upon nothing."

Isaiah 40:22
It is he that sitteth upon **the circle of the earth,** and the inhabitants thereof are as grasshoppers; that stretcheth out the heavens as a curtain, and spreadeth them out as a tent to dwell in.

Back in grade school, I was taught that Columbus discovered America in the year 1492. Before the era of Columbus, it was a common belief that the earth was flat, and if you went far enough in one direction, you would sail off the edge and fall into the abyss. In my Webster's Concise Family Dictionary, the Abyss is described as "the bottomless pit in old accounts of the universe." That fear of falling off the end of the world was a real fear held by most everyone back in the first thousand or more years of recorded history. But when we look at God's divinely inspired words (that are not tampered with) in today's Bible, we see that he said "the circle of the earth." It makes perfect sense to me that the creator of all things would know on day one of recorded history that the earth was round and not flat.

I look to divinely inspired scripture references like the above three to reinforce my belief that God is real and he knows the end from the beginning. Humans may get some things right and some things wrong, but God is always right. If the people in the

What We've Been Told About the Holy Bible is a Lie and Here's the Proof

days before Christopher Columbus would have read this verse from the Bible, and if God would have quickened them in their spirit to open their understanding, then they would have known that the earth was round, like a circle, even before that fact was discovered by scientists later on. If the people who lived before modern science proved that the world was round would have had a personal one on one relationship between them and God, like Abraham had, and read/believed the Bible, they could have saved themselves all that fear of sailing off the edge of the earth and falling into the abyss. Another comment God made to Isaiah (in 40:22) about how we are like grasshoppers that stretch out the heavens like a curtain, and spread them out as a tent to dwell in, could also be taken as a prophecy of how today we are traveling into outer space and looking for another inhabitable planet out there. It was on the news recently that the astronomers may have found a system like ours in space that has its own planet like our Jupiter. Anyway, before I finished my book, I wanted to show that some of the original divinely inspired Bible hasn't been tampered with or interpolated. To me, the above three scripture references are evidence of it.

Epilogue

In the beginning of my book I told you how, after I began discovering the items that I have pointed out to you in this book, I went through the five classic stages of grief as I slowly but surely realized that the Bible that has been my companion, friend, and life blood for several decades has been tampered with and interpolated. Those five stages of grief are: 1) Denial, 2) Anger, 3) Bargaining, 4) Depression, and, finally, 5) Acceptance. It took years before I finally accepted the truth of my discoveries, and arrived at the stage of acceptance. I'm guessing that you too may have a shock to your belief system after you have read the proof in my book about my findings that today's Bible has been interpolated, as I did. In the event that this is the case, I thought I would share a technique that I use to help me understand my feelings. I got some professional help, and I will share with you what my doctor shared with me, in hopes that it will be some benefit to you too. I found that I initiated my feelings, no matter what they are, either good or bad. I do this because of my thoughts and beliefs. Therefore, whenever I have negative emotions, I examine what I was saying to myself in my self-talk just before I felt that emotion. I also identify the activating event that prompted my self-talk, which resulted in the emotions I felt. I learned that if I discover my internal thoughts, even though they are based on my beliefs, are irrational or illogical, then I can change how I feel by changing how and what I think and believe. I will give you an example. Let's say I am standing in the check out line at the grocery store, when the person behind me bumps into my backside with their shopping cart. Even before I turn around to see who did it, I might automatically start thinking, "this dirty, rotten, no good so-and-so isn't watching where they are going, or maybe they bumped into me on purpose". It doesn't take a second for a few thoughts to flutter through my mind between the bump and my turning around to see who did it. If I automatically have negative thoughts like I wrote above, then my feelings would be angry even before I turn around. Then I turn around and see a man with a white cane and dark glasses behind me. Upon my realizing that he is blind, I am no longer angry because I realize he probably didn't bump into me on purpose at all. But why was I angry for that instant between the time he first bumped into me from behind, until I turned around and saw that it was a blind man? I caused myself those angry feelings by my own self-talk. This example is representative of all the feelings you or I feel. There is some activating event. In my example it was the person behind me in the check out line bumping into me with a shopping cart. But it can be any activating event that confronts us in life. It is how I think and believe about that activating event that causes my feelings. Another example to illustrate what I am trying to explain could be a rainy day. If your self-talk upon seeing that it was a rainy day was negative, then you would cause yourself negative feelings. If your self-talk was positive, like telling yourself how good the rain will be for the farmers and gardeners, then your feelings would be positive feelings. I learned this technique from my doctor. If you apply it towards all of your activating events, you can discover if your thoughts and beliefs are rational or irrational. And if they are irrational, you can change how you feel by changing how you choose to think and believe. My explanation here is only a simplified overview of the process involved.

When applying this technique to any negative or scary feelings you may have when you find out that today's Bible has been interpolated, based on the facts that I have pointed out in this book, you can do as I did, and have your self-talk be positive (and believe it). For instance, you could say that maybe Reverend Shaw's book proved there are flaws and errors in today's Bible, but there is a lot of today's Bible that hasn't been tampered with. You could say to yourself that there might even be other divinely inspired books that were considered apocrypha by the Nicene Council that might be helpful to me in my spiritual walk (if they could be located). You could say in your self-talk that maybe today's Bible does have flaws and errors in it, but that is man's fault, not God's. I still have Jesus as my personal Lord and Savior, so I know I am going to heaven when I die and God raises me up in the judgment and brings me into heaven. Self-talk along these lines will result in a more positive feeling, even in the face of realizing that today's Bible has been interpolated from when it was originally divinely inspired by God. After reading this book you could even feel liberated if today's Bible has seemed confusing and contradictory to you, but you were afraid to openly admit it before you read my book. In that case, my book gives you validation and explains why you felt that way (because you were right). By you focusing on positive self-talk (and believing it) you will be able to work through the five stages of grief (as I had to do) and get to acceptance quicker. And if you pay attention to your self-talk (beliefs) and practice this technique in all of your affairs, you will get good at it, and the result will be that you will become a more healthy, well-adjusted, rational human being as you travel along this path of life.

If I had learned this technique early in my life I could have spared myself a lot of bad feelings and hurtful experiences, that I now realize I caused to myself. All I have to do is pay attention.

Before I close, if perchance there are some people who are reading my book that are not Born Again Christians, I would like to invite you to accept Jesus Christ as your own personal Lord and Savior also. I will point out a few Bible scripture references that show us the way to salvation. After that I will give you a prayer you can say to become reborn as a Christian.

Romans 3:10
As it is written, There is none righteous, no, not one.

Romans 3:23
For all have sinned, and come short of the glory of God.

Romans 5:12
Wherefore, as by one man sin entered into the world, and death by sin; and so death passed upon all men, for that all have sinned:

Romans 5:8
But God commendeth his love toward us, in that, while we were yet sinners, Christ died for us.

Romans 6:23
For the wages of sin is death; but the gift of God is eternal life through Jesus Christ our Lord.

Romans 10:13
For whosoever shall call upon the name of the Lord shall be saved.

Revelation 3:20
Behold, I stand at the door, and knock: if any man hear my voice, and open the door, I will come in to him, and will sup with him, and he with me.

Romans 10:9-10
That if thou shalt confess with thy mouth the Lord Jesus, and shalt believe in thine heart that God hath raised him from the dead, thou shalt be saved. For with the heart man believeth unto righteousness; and with the mouth confession is made unto salvation.

The above scripture references tell us that no-one is righteous, that we all have sinned and need to repent and accept salvation. Christ died for our sins so we could accept him and appropriate his shed blood to cover our sins. Then the scripture says that <u>whosoever</u> calls on the name of the Lord <u>shall</u> be saved. Scripture says that if <u>any man</u> asks Jesus to come into their heart, he will come in. The way to become a Born Again Christian is to do what scripture tells us in Romans 10:9-10. Simply confess that Jesus is Lord, believe in your heart that God raised him from the dead, and thou shalt be saved. It is as simple as that. Are you "whosoever?" Are you "any man?" When the Bible says "man" I believe that means any "human." If you want to accept Jesus as your own personal Lord and Savior, follow the above instructions and you <u>shall</u> be saved. It doesn't say "maybe." God's word says you <u>shall</u> be saved. If you aren't a Born Again Christian and you would like to be, repeat the following prayer for salvation.

Prayer for Salvation
Heavenly Father, I come to You in the Name of Jesus. Your Word in Romans 10:13 says "… that whosoever shall call on the name of the Lord shall be saved." I am calling on You. I pray and ask Jesus to come into my heart and be Lord over my life according to Romans 10:9-10, "That if thou shalt confess with thy mouth the Lord Jesus, and shalt believe in thine heart that God hath raised him from the dead, thou shalt be saved." I do that now. I confess that Jesus is Lord, and I believe in my heart that God raised him from the dead.

I am now reborn! I am a Christian; a child of Almighty God! I am saved!

Congratulations! Now continue to grow in your spiritual walk by studying the Bible for yourself, while using my book as a reference to help steer you around the flaws and errors. Find yourself a church where the minister, priest, or televangelist is telling you the truth about the whole Bible, including informing you that parts in the Bible have been interpolated.

In closing, I will share with you four beautiful scripture references that are universally used in closing Benedictions.

Numbers 6: 24-26
The Lord bless thee, and keep thee: The Lord make his face shine upon thee, and be gracious unto thee: The Lord lift up his countenance upon thee, and give thee peace.

2 Corinthians 13:14
The grace of the Lord Jesus Christ, and the love of God, and the communion of the Holy Ghost, be with you all. Amen.

Ephesians 1:2
Grace be to you, and peace, from God our Father, and from the Lord Jesus Christ.

3 John 2
Beloved, I wish above all things that thou mayest prosper and be in health, even as thy soul prospereth.

Before I end my Epilogue, I want to make some final comments with regards to the scripture reference of 3 John 2. I see a built-in condition as to if we get the blessings of prosperity and health from God. It has to do with your soul prospering. If you work on your spiritual walk with God, then your soul will prosper. 3 John 2 says that He wishes above all things that you will prosper and be in health as your soul prospers. I see that as a condition. If you aren't working on your spiritual walk with God, then you will be missing some of God's blessings in the areas of prosperity and health. It might seem as if God is treating one person differently than another, under conditions that appear to be the same. I believe we all can point to someone who seems to be an exception to the rule. But we can't accurately call it on an individual case by case basis because there are too many variables that we can't see (although God can). I believe that in all cases at all times, even in the seemingly paradoxical cases, the scriptures work and do exactly what they say they will do. As an example of an unseen variable that may be affecting someone's spiritual walk, let's look at Mark 11:25-26, Ephesians 4:32, and Galatians 5:6.

Mark 11:25-26
And when ye stand praying, forgive, if ye have ought against any: that your Father also which is in heaven may forgive you your trespasses. But if ye do not forgive, neither will your Father which is in heaven forgive your trespasses.

Ephesians 4:32
And be ye kind one to another, tenderhearted, forgiving one another, even as God for Christ's sake hath forgiven you.

Galatians 5:6
For in Jesus Christ neither circumcision availeth any thing, nor uncircumcision; but faith which worketh by love.

Here we see another case where one thing is contingent on another. We may know a Christian who has faith, yet he or she may be in poor health or may not be prospering. There might be something in that person's heart that we don't see, but God does. It clearly states in Mark 11:25-26 and in Ephesians 4:32 that we need to forgive those who have offended us. The condition is the love that we are supposed to have towards our fellow human beings, (even the unlovable ones). According to Galatians 5:6, if we don't love, then our faith won't work. So let's not be quick to point out a seeming exception to the rule of God's conditions and laws because we don't see it as God sees it, as it tells us in 1 Corinthians 2:11.

1 Corinthians 2:11
For what man knoweth the things of a man, save the spirit of man which is in him? even so the things of God knoweth no man, but the Spirit of God.

We can't see into another person's spiritual path like God can. I believe God's laws work at all times, whether or not we see or understand them, as is reflected in the following scripture reference.

<u>Galatians 6:7</u>
Be not deceived; God is not mocked: for whatsoever a man soweth, that shall he also reap.

Afterword

I have done it. I have informed the clergy who have been intentionally preaching selected parts from the Bible to keep the flock ignorant of the whole truth of the flaws, errors, and interpolations in today's Bible, in order to keep their memberships under their control. I have done my duty and delivered my soul.

Ezekiel 3:17-19
Son of man, I have made thee a watchman unto the house of Israel: therefore hear the word at my mouth, and give them warning from me. When I say unto the wicked, Thou shalt surely die; and thou givest him not warning, nor speakest to warn the wicked from his wicked way, to save his life; the same wicked man shall die in his iniquity; but his blood will I require at thine hand. Yet if thou warn the wicked, and he turn not from his wickedness, nor from his wicked way, he shall die in his iniquity; but thou hast delivered thy soul.

To Order More Books

If you would like to order Reverend Shaw's book, <u>What We've Been Told About the HOLY BIBLE is a Lie and Here's the Proof</u>, as a gift to a friend, relative, or for your clergy, just write or call the Trafford Publishing numbers below.

Book sales for North America
<u>Trafford Publishing,</u>
1663 Liberty Drive
Bloomington, IN 47403
toll-free: 1 888 232 4444 (USA & Canada)
phone: 250 383 6864 ◆ fax: 812 355 4082
email: info@trafford.com

Order online at:
www.trafford.com

Co-publisher:
F.V. Westover Trust Publishing
P. O. Box 905
LaCrosse, WI 54602-0905 USA

About the Author

Reverend Shaw was born a Christian (Catholic). Twenty-five years ago he had a Spiritual Awakening and became a Saved (Born Again) Sanctified, filled with the Holy Spirit, and remains so to this day. In his book, Reverend Shaw purposely didn't name the various Bible Colleges that he graduated from during the past dozen years, because due to the tone and content of his book, he didn't want to cast aspersion on any of them. Reverend Shaw is retired. Upon waking at 5 a.m. (without an alarm clock) he spends his first hour of every day in prayer and meditation with God, including weekdays, weekends, and holidays, 365 days a year. He says he has to put on THE FULL ARMOR OF GOD (Ephesians 6:10-18) before the commotion of the day begins. Then throughout the day until bedtime, he touches base with God through short prayers and thanksgiving. He calls them his continuing "popcorn" prayers with God. For the past twenty years Reverend Shaw has been a single, celibate, non-smoker and non-drinker. For his leisure time activities, Reverend Shaw enjoys swimming, stamp collecting, photography, hand-tooling and dyeing his own leather belts and wallets, reading, gardening, bird watching, painting, bee-keeping, doing crossword puzzles,

Sudoku, and anagrams, watching old black & white classic movies, and taking walks. Besides God's Grace, Reverend Shaw attributes his 170 cholesterol and 120/80 blood pressure to being a partial vegetarian (except for fish and fowl). Being retired, Reverend Shaw is finally able to devote his time to pursuing his life-long dream of slowly and meticulously organizing, developing, and writing this book and other books in the privacy and solitude of his own retreat.

Would You Like Reverend Shaw to Personally Intercede Before God in Prayer for Your ecific Need?

Reverend Shaw will be glad to personally lift up your specific need in prayer before God and intercede on your behalf. Reverend Shaw has a personal one-on-one relationship with God, in his daily personal dialogue with God. Reverend Shaw has agreed to pray with God for anyone who writes in with their prayer request. If you want Reverend Shaw to stand in the gap for you before God and plead your case, simply write to Reverend Shaw at the co-publisher's address below and state your specific need. It can be any need whatsoever. It can be for a specific area of sickness that you or a loved one has, the salvation of yourself, a spouse, child, relative or friend. It can be for depression, suicidal thoughts, anger, alcoholism or drug addiction, or for a job that you need. It can be for deliverance from nicotine, caffeine, red meat, lying, profanity, pornography, infidelity, gambling or any other addiction that you or a loved one has and would like to be set free of. If you or someone you know needs an exorcism to be set free from demon possession or any evil spirit, just write to Reverend Shaw at the co-publisher's address below and lay out your specific need to him in your letter. We will be sure that Reverend Shaw gets your prayer request forwarded to him, and Reverend Shaw will fervently go before God in your behalf and pray for your specific need, binding and loosing SPIRIT-FILLED PRAYER IN THE NAME OF JESUS!!!

1 Timothy 5:17-18

If you choose to write to Reverend Shaw with your prayer request need, please use the address below. Reverend Shaw will freely pray for your needs. Reverend Shaw would not refuse to pray for anyone regardless of their situation. He prays on his uplink with God for others based only on their prayer need, and nothing else.
Co-publisher:
F.V. Westover Trust Publishing
P. O. Box 905
LaCrosse, WI 54602-0905 USA

Another One of Reverend Shaw's Books
That is Available:
The SHAW'S REVISED KING JAMES BIBLE

Because of Reverend Shaw's book, <u>What We've Been Told About the HOLY BIBLE is a Lie and Here's the Proof</u>, all of today's Bibles that you own are obsolete. Reverend Shaw, under the same divine inspiration that prompted him to write this book, has made revisions and amendments to correct the flaws, errors, and interpolations that are in today's Bible, as Reverend Shaw has pointed out in this book. Reverend Shaw has made these same amendments in today's Bible as inspired by God's Holy Spirit. <u>The SHAW'S REVISED KING JAMES BIBLE</u> will be the only appropriately corrected revised Bible available on the market today. Every sincere and genuine Christian will need to own a <u>SHAW'S REVISED KING JAMES BIBLE</u> if they want to have a Bible that is free of the flaws, errors, and interpolations that were revealed in Reverend Shaw's book, <u>What We've Been Told About the HOLY BIBLE is a Lie and Here's the Proof</u>.

Since our Circuit, State and Federal court system cannot swear in witnesses TO TELL THE TRUTH, THE WHOLE TRUTH AND NOTHING BUT THE TRUTH, on any of the former Bibles that Dr. Shaw's first book, <u>What We've Been Told About the HOLY BIBLE is a Lie and Here's the Proof</u>, has proven to have errors and mistakes, all the court systems throughout the world of jurisprudence need to change over to and have their witnesses swear in on <u>The Shaw's Revised King James HOLY BIBLE</u>.

If you would like to order the <u>SHAW'S REVISED KING JAMES BIBLE</u> for yourself, or as a gift to a friend, relative or clergyman, just write or call the Trafford Publishing numbers below.

Book sales for North America and international:
Trafford Publishing
1663 Liberty Drive
Bloomington, IN 47403
toll-free: 1 888 232 4444 (USA & Canada)
phone: 250 383 6864 ♦ fax: 812 355 4082
email: info@trafford.com

Order online at:
www.trafford.com

Co-publisher:
F.V. Westover Trust Publishing
P. O. Box 905
LaCrosse, WI 54602-0905 USA

Reverend Shaw's Future Anthology Book Project

One of the next book projects of Reverend Shaw's will be an ANTHOLOGY of some of the correspondence received in response to his book, <u>What We've Been Told About the HOLY BIBLE is a Lie and Here's the Proof</u>. Out of all the letters that Reverend Shaw receives, he will personally respond to some through the co-publisher in his own handwriting. Those who receive replies from Reverend Shaw will also receive (through the co-publisher) a Certificate of Authenticity. Think of what it would be like if you had a handwritten, personal letter from Martin Luther, with a Certificate of Authenticity that it was indeed Martin Luther's personal handwritten letter to you. Martin Luther was born in 1453, and died in Eiselben in 1546. Martin Luther is the father of the Lutheran/Protestant segments of the Christian faith. Luther split with the Roman Catholic church of that time. It is said that he nailed his list of issues with the Roman Catholic church to the front door of the church. Reverend Shaw's book that outlines his problems with today's Bible debunks that Bible. Reverend Shaw's book is bound to be seen in a revolutionary light in the future, somewhat similar to how Martin Luther split with the Roman Catholic church in his day, back in 1517. It would be a prized treasure to have a hand written personal letter from Martin Luther to take and have appraised today on the Antiques Roadshow, Christies, or Sothebys. Therefore, for those of you who would like to have a possibility of being responded to by Reverend Shaw in his own handwriting, as a treasured keepsake in your family, write to Reverend Shaw at the co-publisher's address below.

\Reverend Shaw is only, and freely, interested in the use of the correspondence for his next ANTHOLOGY book project. Unless otherwise requested, Dr. Shaw will consider all letters for inclusion in his next book.

Co-publisher:
F.V. Westover Trust Publishing
P. O. Box 905
LaCrosse, WI 54602-0905 USA

Sources:

WEBSITES:

Collins, Kenneth W., Rev., 2002.
http://www.kencollins.com,bible-c1.htm

Grosswirth, Raymond. List of Married Popes, 8,9,2001.
http://www.inclusivechurch.org, disc other/00 000199.htm

The Forbidden Books of the New Testament. The Marley Store.
http://www.themarleystore.com/forbookofnew .html

CITI – Celibacy is the Issue. An International Married Roman
Catholic Priest Faith Community and The "Rent A Priest"©
Referral Program. CITI, Inc., 1997.
http://www.rentapriest.com/married popes.ht m

BOOKS:

Bokenkotter, Thomas. A Concise History of the Catholic Church.
Image Books, 1990.

Jenkins, Philip. Hidden Gospels: How the Search for Jesus Lost
Its Way. Oxford, England: Oxford University Press, 2001.

Larson, Martin A. The Story of Christian Origins; or The Sources
and Establishment of Western Religion. Tahlequah, OK: Village
Press, 1977.

Latourette, Kenneth Scott. A History of Christianity. Vol. I: to
A.D. 1500. NY: HarperSanFrancisco, 1975.